INFO

INFORMATION GOVERNANCE

GOV

CONCEPTS | REQUIREMENTS | TECHNOLOGIES

WILLIAM SAFFADY, PH.D.

Consulting Editor: Mary L. Ginn, Ph.D.
Composition: Cole Design & Production
Cover Art: Brett Dietrich

ARMA International
11880 College Blvd., Ste 450
Overland Park, KS 66210
913.341.3808

Perfect Bound: A5033 978-1-936654-76-5
PDF: V5033 978-1-936654-77-2

Contents

Preface

Governance is a well-established concept. The *Oxford English Dictionary*, citing references that date from the fourteenth century, defines it as the action or manner of governing, in the sense of directing and controlling with the authority of a superior. The *Macmillan English Dictionary, American Heritage Dictionary of the English Language, Cambridge Academic Content Dictionary*, and the *Oxford Advanced Learners' Dictionary* provide similar definitions. The *Miriam-Webster Dictionary* defines governance as the way that an entity is controlled by the people who run it. The *Random House Dictionary* equates governance with a method or system of management.

As a noun, governance is often modified by an adjective that indicates the entity or activity being governed or the context in which governance occurs. The most common example is corporate governance, a phrase that has been in use for decades. According to the *Report of the Committee on the Financial Aspects of Corporate Governance*—an influential source that is popularly known as the Cadbury Report—corporate governance is the system by which companies are directed and controlled.[1] This definition is the customary starting point for published discussions of corporate governance, all of which emphasize the importance of strategic direction and internal controls to support organizational objectives.[2] While the concept of corporate governance initially applied to for-profit businesses, journal articles, conference papers, and other publications have broadened its scope to encompass educational and cultural institutions, scientific and technical

---

[1] The Cadbury Report was issued in the United Kingdom in December 1992 by a committee chaired by Sir Adrian Cadbury, a former Chairman of Cadbury Schweppes and a director of the Bank of England. The full report as published by Gee and Co., Ltd. is available online at *www.ecgi.org/codes/documents/cadbury.pdf*.

[2] Examples of publications that have adopted the Cadbury Report's definition of corporate governance include the *OECD Glossary of Statistical Terms*, a comprehensive set of definitions assembled by the Organization for Economic Cooperation and Development; the *G20/OECD Principles of Corporate Governance*, the latest version of an international benchmark that was first issued in 1999; and various international standards, including ISO/IEC 38500, *Information Technology—Governance of IT for the Organization*, ISO/IEC TR 38502, *Information Technology—Governance of IT—Framework and Model*, ISO 21500, *Guidance on Project Management*, and ISO/IEC 27000, *Information Technology—Security Techniques—Information Security Management Systems—Overview and Vocabulary*.

research organizations, professional associations, philanthropic foundations, community-based organizations, religious groups, and other not-for-profit entities.

Information governance is a focused aspect of corporate governance but, compared to corporate governance, it is a newer concept. The phrase's first appearance in the title of books and journal articles dates from the early 2000s, but its usage has increased significantly since that time. In mid-2016, the ABI Inform database, a leading indexing source for business magazines and journals, listed over 515 articles that contain the phrase "information governance" in the title or full text. A Google phrase search for information governance retrieved approximately 536,000 web entries, 15,000 news entries, 10,500 book entries, and 27,800 videos, many of them vendor presentations. A Google Scholar search retrieved over 7,600 publications that contain the phrase.

This book is intended for records managers, attorneys and other legal information specialists, compliance officers, risk management specialists, auditors, information management consultants, data scientists, archivists, librarians, and other decision-makers, managers, and analysts who are involved in information-related activities or who are responsible for or affected by their organizations' information governance initiatives. The book can also be used as a textbook by colleges and universities that offer courses in information governance or related topics at the graduate or advanced undergraduate level. In particular, the book may be useful for a curriculum that combines information governance with records management, knowledge management, information science, health informatics, and other information-related subjects.

The book is divided into three parts:

- *Part 1 provides an introduction to information governance concepts.* It defines key terms, explains the business case for information governance as a strategic initiative, surveys governance frameworks, and discusses the roles, responsibilities, and interactions of information governance stakeholders. It also describes related governance initiatives and explains the role of maturity analysis in planning and assessing an organization's information governance program.

- *Part 2 surveys legal and regulatory requirements that affect information governance stakeholders and initiatives.* The survey covers recordkeeping requirements, data protection and privacy requirements, information security requirements, information disclosure requirements, and statutes of limitations. For each category, the survey summarizes and cites examples of typical laws and regulations and explains their impact on information governance.

- *Part 3 examines technologies that are important for information governance initiatives.* The discussion covers technologies that organize, analyze, and categorize information; technologies that manage the information lifecycle; technologies that retrieve information; and technologies that address risk management and information security requirements. The discussion describes the most important characteristics of each technology and assesses its impact on information governance stakeholders and requirements.

Throughout the book, the treatment of information governance is practical rather than theoretical. Published standards are cited where applicable. A comparison of governance models, a responsibility assignment matrix, and stakeholder and technology matrices are included in *Appendixes A–D*. Although terms and concepts are defined when first introduced in the text, *Appendix E* provides a glossary of important definitions for convenient reference. *Appendix F* contains suggestions for finding additional information about information governance concepts, requirements, and technologies.

Information Governance Concepts

All organizational initiatives have governance requirements. Information-related initiatives, which are indispensable components of virtually all organizational activities, are not exempt. The purpose, scope, and characteristics of information governance have been defined by professional associations, researchers, consultants, vendors, and others:

- To date, the only standardized definition relates to healthcare information. ISO/TR 11633-1, *Health Informatics—Information Security Management for Remote Maintenance of Medical Devices and Medical Information Systems—Part 1: Requirements and Risk Analysis*, defines *information governance* as the "processes by which an organization obtains assurance that the risks to its information, and thereby the operational capabilities and integrity of the organization, are effectively identified and managed."[3]

- ARMA International's *Glossary of Records Management and Information Governance Terms* defines **information governance** as "a strategic, cross-disciplinary framework composed of standards, processes, roles, and metrics that hold organizations and individuals accountable for the proper handling of information assets. The framework helps organizations achieve business objectives, facilitates compliance with external requirements, and minimizes risk posed by substandard information handling practices."

- According to the Gartner IT Glossary,[4] a widely cited web-based source for technology terms, *information governance* is "the specification of decision rights and an accountability framework to ensure appropriate behavior in the valuation,

---

[3] The same definition is presented in other health informatics standards, including ISO/TR 11633-2, *Health Informatics—Information Security Management for Remote Maintenance of Medical Devices and Medical Information Systems—Part 2: Implementation of an Information Security Management System (ISMS)*; ISO/TS 13972, *Health Informatics—Detailed Clinical Models, Characteristics, and Processes*; ISO/TS 14441, *Health Informatics—Security and Privacy Requirements of HER Systems for Use in Conformity Assessment*, and ISO/TS 14265, *Health Informatics—Classification of Purposes for Processing Personal Health Information*.

[4] *http://www.gartner.com/it-glossary/*.

creation, storage, use, archiving, and deletion of information. It includes the processes, roles and policies, standards, and metrics that ensure the effective and efficient use of information in enabling an organization to achieve its goals."

- Acknowledging both ARMA International and Gartner, the American Health Information Management Association (AHIMA) defines *information governance* as "an organization-wide framework for managing information throughout its lifecycle and supporting the organization's strategy, operations, regulatory, legal, risk, and environmental requirements."

- The Sedona Conference®, a research and educational institute that focuses on law and policy issues, defines *information governance* as "an organization's coordinated, interdisciplinary approach to satisfying information legal and compliance requirements and managing information risks while optimizing information value."[5]

- The Information Governance Initiative, a cross-disciplinary consortium, defines *information governance* as "the activities and technologies that organizations employ to maximize the value of their information while minimizing associated risks and costs."[6]

- According to the Digital Clarity Group, a provider of technology analysis and strategic advice, *information governance* is "all the rules, regulations, legislation, standards, and policies with which organizations need to comply when they create, share, and use information."[7]

- IBM defines *information governance* as "a holistic approach to managing and leveraging information for business benefits and encompasses information quality, information protection and information life cycle management."[8]

While these definitions differ in length and some details, they collectively delineate key characteristics of an information governance program and highlight its distinctive contribution to organizational governance:

- Information governance determines how an organization's information-related initiatives will be conducted.

- Information governance creates a strategic framework that aligns information-related initiatives with an organization's mission.

- Information governance defines information-related roles, decision-making authority, and accountability.

- Information governance establishes standards for information-related initiatives.

- Information governance has a multi-disciplinary perspective that facilitates collaboration and cooperation to support information-related initiatives.

- Information governance emphasizes compliance with legal and regulatory requirements related to the creation, storage, retention, reliability, usability, long-term accessibility, distribution, and protection of information.

- Information governance reduces an organization's exposure to information-related risks.

- Information governance promotes processes and technologies that maximize the cost-effective utilization and value of an organization's information assets.

[5] *The Sedona Conference® Commentary on Information Governance.* Phoenix, AZ: The Sedona Conference®, 2013.

[6] *Information Governance Initiative: Annual Report 2015-2016.* http://iginitiative.com/wp-content/uploads/2015_IGI-Annual-Report_Final-digital-use.pdf.

[7] Chris Walker, *Information Governance Is,* July 16, 2014. http://www.digitalclaritygroup.com/information-governance-is/.

[8] Judith R. Davis, *Information Governance as a Holistic Approach to Managing and Leveraging Information.* BeyeNetwork Custom Research Report Prepared for IBM Corporation, 2010. *ftp://public.dhe.ibm.com/software/os/systemz/IBM_Information_Governance_Survey_Report.pdf.* In a slight variation, IBM defines data governance as "a holistic approach to managing, improving, and leveraging information to help you gain insight and build confidence in business decisions and operations." *http://www.ibm.com/analytics/us/en/technology/data-governance/.*

Definitions rarely capture all aspects of a complex activity. Useful as the previous definitions are, some important elements are missing. Senior executive involvement, an essential component of corporate governance and a critical factor for a successful information governance implementation, is not mentioned. The definitions do not mention control, planning, prioritization, and oversight, all of which are well-established aspects of governance initiatives. While they list the information-related activities—retention, storage, regulatory compliance, and so on—that are covered by information governance, the definitions do not consider the relationship of information governance to existing information-related disciplines, such as records management and information technology, that have been performing those activities for decades. Most importantly, the definitions do not address the relationship of information governance to an organization's existing information-related functions and governance initiatives, most of which predate information governance. Although information governance is closely allied to these functions and governance initiatives, it must be something more than the sum of its parts, and it must deliver value that an organization's existing information-related environment and operations cannot provide. These points are discussed in the following sections.

The Business Case

A convincing statement of business value is a precondition for acceptance of any governance initiative. A longstanding acknowledgment among business executives is that effective corporate governance adds value to an organization.

A widely cited survey conducted by McKinsey & Company in cooperation with the Global Corporate Governance Forum found that global investors put effective corporate governance on a par with profit, growth, and other financial indicators when making investment decisions.[9] A majority of the participating investors were willing to pay a premium ranging from 12 percent to more than 30 percent for well-governed companies.

This relationship between effective governance and increased valuation is straightforward. Effective governance involves close monitoring and transparency, which increase confidence and decrease the perception of risk. In particular, effective governance increases the likelihood that an organization will act diligently and prudently when making decisions about the acquisition, maintenance, use, and disposition of assets. Responsibility of governance for stewardship of assets is forcefully stated in *Corpus Juris Secundum*, a comprehensive legal encyclopedia that presents the principles of U.S. law as derived from legislation and reported cases. According to Volume 19, Section 491, an organization's officers have a duty

---

[9] *Global Investor Opinion Survey on Corporate Governance.* Boston, MA: McKinsey & Company, 2002. *http://www.eiod.org/uploads/Publications/Pdf/II-Rp-4-1.pdf.*

"to be vigilant and to exercise ordinary or reasonable care and diligence and the utmost good faith and fidelity to conserve the corporate property; and, if a loss or depletion of assets results from their willful or negligent failure to perform their duties, or to a willful or fraudulent abuse of their trust, they are liable, provided such losses were the natural and necessary consequences of omission on their part." According to the previously cited Cadbury Report, governance encourages "the efficient use of resources" and requires "accountability for the stewardship of those resources."

Governance mechanisms enable an organization to fulfill these duties, which are ultimately the responsibility of a board of directors, board of trustees, or other governing body. Initiatives and activities that facilitate the work of an organization's governing body make a direct contribution to value. As a specialized component of an organization's governance structure, information governance's distinctive contribution to value is based on the role of information as an organizational asset.

Information as an Asset

ISO 55000, *Asset management—Overview, principles and terminology*, defines an **asset** as an "item, thing or entity that has potential or actual value to an organization." The ISO definition notes that an asset's value may be tangible or intangible, financial or nonfinancial, and positive or negative, and that the value of an asset may vary at different stages of the life of the asset. In financial accounting, an asset is broadly defined as an economic resource that has value. Obvious examples of organizational assets include cash and cash equivalents, long-term investments, real property, inventory, equipment, and accounts receivable.

The International Accounting Standards Board's conceptual framework for financial reporting characterizes an asset as a resource that is controlled by an entity as a result of past events and from which future economic benefits are expected to flow to the entity. Information possesses those characteristics:

- Information is controlled by the organization that owns it. The organization decides how and when information will be used.

- Information is the result of prior events or transactions that caused the information to be created, collected, or discovered.

- Information is capable of producing economic benefits through sale or use. The benefits may be realized immediately or at some future time.

Writing in the September 24, 1992, issue of *The Wall Street Journal*, Peter Drucker noted that the economy of developed countries was increasingly organized around the flow of information rather than the flow of things or money.[10] The Hawley Committee, a group of high-level executives from the financial, retail, and security industries in the United Kingdom, was among the first authorities to characterize information as an asset that should be under the control and governance of an

---

[10]   Peter Drucker, "The Economy's Power Shift," *The Wall Street Journal*, Eastern Edition, September 24, 1992.

organization's board of directors. Issued in 1995, the Committee's report[11] cited types of information that have value as assets, including customer information, product information, specialist knowledge, business process information, management information on which decisions are based, human resources information, supplier information, and legal and regulatory information. In the same year, Reuters Business Information reported the findings of 500 telephone interviews with senior managers in the United Kingdom.[12] Twenty-five percent of the interviewees considered information to be their organization's most important asset, but some respondents indicated that it was difficult to measure its value.

Measuring Asset Value

Valuation is the process of estimating what an asset is worth in monetary terms. The value of an asset can be measured in several ways:

- **Historical cost.** Valuation can be based on the original cost to acquire an asset. This method, which reflects the value of the asset at the time it was obtained, is a traditional accounting approach to valuation. It is based on a straightforward premise: the historical cost of an asset must accurately reflect its perceived value, or the organization that acquired the asset would not have been willing to incur that cost. For information assets, the historical cost to create and collect information is the most practical and broadly applicable approach to valuation.

- **Value-in-exchange.** Valuation can be based on the amount that others are willing to pay for an asset. For information assets, this value-in-exchange method is generally limited to specific items—such as intellectual property, technical information, or market research data—that may be sold or licensed to other organizations. The value-in-exchange concept is not applicable to other information. For the most part, an organization's general administrative information or information about expired business transactions has little market value. In some jurisdictions, the sale of information about an organization's employees or customers, which might be of interest for marketing or other purposes, is prohibited by privacy and data protection laws or regulations. Even where it is applicable to information assets, value-in-exchange can be difficult to measure. Given the unique characteristics of an organization's information and the fact that it is seldom sold, valuation cannot be based on the sale of comparable items, an approach that is widely used to appraise art works, real estate, and other assets.[13]

---

[11] *Information as an Asset: The Board Agenda—a Consultative Report.* London: KPMG IMPACT Programme, 1995. The Committee was chaired by Dr. Robert Hawley, the chief executive of Nuclear Power plc.

[12] *Information as an Asset: The Invisible Goldmine—A Report Exploring the Current and Future Value of Information in Business.* London: Reuters Business Information, 1995.

[13] Exceptions are made for publishing companies, data aggregators, information distributors, and other organizations that create or collect information expressly for sale and for the personal papers of famous authors, artists, and other celebrities, which may be purchased by libraries, universities, museums, historical societies, or other research organizations.

- **Value-in-use.** Valuation can be based on the future economic benefits that an asset is expected to confer. Measurement of future benefits is typically limited to information that is associated with specific activities or business operations. The value-in-use approach is often used to justify the implementation of new technologies or methodologies, which may reduce an organization's operating costs or increase its revenues. In such situations, the resulting valuation relates to the efficient management of information as an operational asset rather than to its governance as a strategic asset. As a significant limitation of this valuation method, the anticipated future benefits may never be realized.

Historical cost is a useful valuation measure for an organization's information assets, but it is not easy to determine. No comprehensive surveys of the total cost that an organization of a given type incurs to create and collect information is available, but various studies provide useful estimates of the historical cost of specific information-related initiatives and activities. Given the high percentage of information that is created, collected, and stored in digital format, estimates of information technology expenditures provide a useful starting point for valuation of information assets based on historical cost.

A 2015 member survey by the Society for Information Management (SIM International) found that information technology spending in 785 organizations averaged 5.3 percent of revenue as compared with 5.15 percent in 2014 and 3.55 percent in 2011.[14] According to a survey of information technology executives published in January 2015 by *CIO* magazine, information technology budgets averaged 6.3 percent of revenue in 2014, a decrease from 8.6 percent in the previous year but higher than the 5.2 percent reported in 2012. Some sources cite lower percentages. A study by Computer Economics, for example, estimates information technology spending at 2.3 percent of revenues, a decrease from 2.5 percent in each of the two prior years, but it notes that information technology spending is a higher percentage of revenues in the financial services, retail, and healthcare sectors.[15] According to the IT Dashboard, a U.S. government website,[16] the information technology budgets of federal agencies exceeded $79.5 billion for the 2016 budget year. This amount represents about 3.3 percent of annual federal government revenues, excluding social security and other payroll taxes.

Information technology expenditures are typically limited to computer and communications equipment, software, IT department staff, and purchased IT services. Estimates based on those expenditures omit the cost of labor expended by an organization's business units and functional areas to create and collect information in digital and nondigital formats. According to the Kaiser Family Foundation, 58 million employees—about 40 percent of the U.S. workforce—are considered

---

[14] *SIM IT Trends Study Comprehensive Report.* Leon Kappelman, Primary Investigator. Mount Laurel, NJ: SIM International, 2015.

[15] *IT Spending & Staffing Benchmarks: 2015.* Irvine, CA: Computer Economics, 2015.

[16] *www.itdashboard.gov.*

professionals or managers.[17] If each of these employees spends just two hours each day generating reports, responding to email messages, and otherwise creating or collecting information at an average salary of $35 per hour—admittedly, many professionals and managers are paid more and spend more time creating information—their contribution to the historical cost of information exceeds one trillion dollars. This estimate does not include the labor cost of clerical and administrative employees who spend many working hours creating and collecting information about transactions or other business operations. According to the Bureau of Labor Statistics, over 13 million employees work in clerical and administrative positions in the United States.[18]

Human resources specialists typically recommend that payroll costs equal 15 to 30 percent of an organization's revenue. At that rate, the labor cost of employees who spend 25 percent of their work day creating or collecting information will equal 3.75 to 7.5 percent of an organization's revenue. When labor costs are considered, the historical cost of information in developed countries likely exceeds 10 percent of an organization's annual revenues. For a medium-size organization with $25 million in annual revenue, for example, the estimated value of information assets created and collected in a given year exceeds $2.5 million; for a billion-dollar corporation, the estimated value exceeds $100 million per year. Based on these calculations, the historical cost of information assets is similar to the historical cost of some other organizational assets of comparable importance. As an example, the APQC, a not-for-profit organization that deals with business benchmarking and best practices, estimates the median value of a company's inventory at 10.6 percent of revenue.[19]

Adding Value to Organizational Governance

The preceding discussion confirms that information is a highly valued organizational asset. Viewed in that light, information governance is not merely a good idea; it is an obligation. Information governance enables organizational governance to fulfill its responsibility for prudent stewardship of assets. In particular, information governance adds value by supporting organizational governance in the following areas:

• **Strategic alignment.** All governance mechanisms must address the so-called principal-agent problem in which the actions of a department, subsidiary, or other organizational unit (the agent) are not aligned with the interests of the

---

[17] *http://kff.org/other/state-indicator/blue-and-white-collar-workers/.*

[18] *Occupational Outlook Handbook,* 2014-15 Edition. Washington, DC: Bureau of Labor Statistics, U.S. Department of Labor, 2014.

[19] Ultimately, information may have a higher valuation than inventory. According to the Council of Supply Chain Management Professionals, inventory costs were equivalent to 8.3 percent of GDP in 2014 but, as recently as 2010, inventory costs were equivalent to 14.1 percent of GDP. (See Rosalyn Wilson, *26th Annual "State of Logistics Report®".* Lombard, IL: Council of Supply Chain Management Professionals, 2015). The reduction is largely attributed to organizational investments in information systems that support more efficient inventory management—a tradeoff that is sometimes characterized as "information for inventory."

organization as a whole (the principal). This lack of alignment can squander assets, obstruct operations, and prevent an organization from capitalizing on opportunities. To prevent this situation from occurring, a governing body must use policy and oversight to align local practices with enterprise-wide requirements and priorities. Information governance supports this strategic alignment. If organizational strategy emphasizes centralized services to achieve economies of scale and uniform practices, for example, information governance will promote consolidated information technology operations, enterprise-wide records retention guidance, and other centralized information-related initiatives. On the other hand, if an organization wants to maintain local autonomy of subsidiaries and business functions to make divesting them or accommodating special operational requirements easier, information governance will emphasize decentralization of information technology, local development of records retention policies, and other initiatives tailored to local implementation.

- **Compliance.** According to the American Bar Association,[20] an organization's governing body must ensure compliance with laws and regulations. As discussed in Part 2 of this book, various laws and regulations contain recordkeeping requirements, limitations on collection or disclosure of specific types of information, restrictions on geographic locations where information can be stored, and other information-related provisions. Information governance enables an organization's governing body to fulfill its compliance-related responsibilities by identifying laws and regulations that deal with information-related matters and aligning organizational policies, procedures, and practices with legal and regulatory requirements. Information governance is also concerned with compliance with organizational codes of conduct and other internal mandates that relate to information assets. As discussed later in this chapter, all information governance stakeholders are involved with compliance-related matters to some extent.

- **Risk. Risk** is the effect of uncertainty on objectives, often expressed as a combination of the adverse consequences of an event and the likelihood of occurrence of the event. As discussed in a 2009 report by the National Association of Corporate Directors (NACD), a governing body must understand, evaluate, and monitor an organization's risk exposure.[21] **Risk management** includes coordinated activities to direct and control an organization with regard to risk. The Financial Reporting Council, which maintains the United Kingdom's corporate governance and stewardship codes, emphatically states that a governing body "has responsibility for an organization's overall approach to risk management."[22] Information governance supports this responsibility by

---

[20] Corporate Laws Committee, American Bar Association Business Law Section. *Corporate Director's Guidebook*, Sixth Edition. Chicago: ABA Publishing, 2011.

[21] *Report of the NACD Blue Ribbon Commission on Risk Governance: Balancing Risk and Reward.* Washington, DC: National Association of Corporate Directors, 2009.

[22] *Guidance on Risk Management, Internal Control and Related Financial and Business Reporting.* London: Financial Reporting Council, 2014.

developing effective strategies and policies to identify, assess, and address risks associated with creation, collection, processing, storage, use, and distribution of information; by defining roles and responsibilities for evaluation, mitigation, and elimination of information-related risks; and by facilitating the collaboration of stakeholders to direct, coordinate, and monitor an organization's responses to specific information-related risks. As with compliance, all information governance stakeholders are involved with risk to some extent.

• **Internal Controls.** The COSO framework—developed by the Committee of Sponsoring Organizations (COSO) of the Treadway Commission, a joint initiative that deals with critical aspects of organizational governance—emphasizes a governing body's responsibility for understanding, assessing, and monitoring an organization's internal controls, including policies and processes for financial controls and disclosure controls. COSO defines **internal controls** as ongoing tasks and activities that are "designed to provide reasonable assurance regarding the achievement of objectives relating to operations, reporting, and compliance."[23] According to the COSO framework, information is "necessary for the entity to carry out internal control responsibilities." By ensuring that information will be controlled by systematically developed policies, guidelines, and standards rather than by the discretionary decisions and actions of individual employees, an information governance program supports a control environment.

Various journal articles, conference presentations, case studies, and other sources cite economic benefits associated with information governance, including cost-effective management of the information lifecycle, more efficient use of information technology resources, improved access to information for transaction processing and decision making, greater security of information, reduced cost of discovery for litigation, and improved compliance with legal and regulatory requirements. Information governance may facilitate these economic benefits, but they are typically delivered by other information-related disciplines and business functions in the context of specific projects or operations. In many cases, those disciplines and functions predate information governance and do not necessarily depend on it. Records management, for example, has a multidecade track record of cost-effective retention initiatives; information technology units have a well-established history of optimizing the implementation and operation of computing and communication resources; the **information security** function implements measures to prevent data breaches for the preservation of confidentiality, authenticity, reliability, and availability of information; the litigation support function implements procedures, technologies, and services to expedite and control the cost of legal discovery; and so on.

This point highlights the difference between governance and management. Governance is concerned with vision and purpose; management is responsible for operations and performance. Governance is sometimes characterized as the

---

[23] *Internal Control—Integrated Framework.* Durham, NC: American Institute of Certified Public Accountants, 2013.

management of managers—a description that accurately conveys the relationship between information governance and information management. Through strategic alignment and stakeholder collaboration, information governance creates an environment in which information management can deliver economic benefits, but information governance's contribution to such benefits is not easily quantified. Differential analysis and return on investment calculations, the two methods most often used to justify information-related investments are not applicable to information governance. Those cost-justification methods are intended for information management projects where initial expenditures will be recaptured through cost reductions or increased revenues over a reasonably short period of time. They are not well suited to ongoing programs. In any case, the implementation of an information governance program typically involves modest initial costs.

Governance Frameworks

*A **governance framework** includes the strategies, policies, decision-making structures, and accountabilities through which an organization's governance arrangements operate.*

This definition is presented in ISO/IEC TR 38502, *Information Technology—Governance of IT—Framework and Model*, but it applies to all forms of governance. Effective governance requires a sound framework.

All governance frameworks include a board, committee, or other group that directs and oversees an organization's activities. To be effective, a governing board must work closely with but not supplant an organization's management. It must have a stable membership that is knowledgeable about the organization and represents the interests of stakeholders. Equally important, a governing board must function as a cohesive unit to support and advance the organization's mission, strategies, and priorities.

Various models define a governing board's authority and its relationship to an organization's management and operational units. These models were originally developed for boards of directors in corporations and not-for-profit organizations that are required by law or their own bylaws to have a governing body, but they have been successfully applied to other governance initiatives. The following sections describe the principal characteristics of five governing board models that are relevant for information governance programs. The models differ in their definition of the governing board's role and its relationship to management. The suitability of a given model depends on a number of factors, including an organization's size, stakeholder interests, and corporate culture. The models are not mutually exclusive. An information governance program may benefit by combining the characteristics of several models.

Executive-centered Model

Drawing on classical theories of organizational management, the executive-led governance model emphasizes top-down control and concentrated authority:

• An organization's governing board is led by an executive officer who is a voting member of the board.

- The executive officer sets the governing board's agenda, and brings issues to the board for consideration. The executive officer guides the governing board and directs its deliberations and activities.

- The governing board's size and composition vary from organization to organization. In some cases, the executive officer selects board members. At its best, this approach promotes participation by key stakeholders and increases the likelihood that members will be able to work together in a cohesive and collegial way, but it may result in a board that is reluctant to challenge the executive officer.

- The executive-centered approach is less collaborative than other governance models discussed next. Its effectiveness is principally determined by the capabilities of one person who is at the top of the leadership hierarchy and has a high level of autonomy. While the governing board has decision-making authority and is nominally independent, it is subordinate to the executive officer in fact if not in theory.

- The executive-centered model does not clearly separate governance from management. As the leader of the board and the leader of the organization, the executive officer both governs and manages.

In results-based governance, a variation of the executive-driven model, a governing board works closely with the executive officer to define the organization's strategic priorities, objectives, and expected results. The executive officer sets the governing board's agenda and participates in meetings as a nonvoting member. As its principal responsibility, the governing board monitors the organization's efficiency and effectiveness in achieving specified outcomes. Although the board and executive officer have a strong partnership, the line between governance and management is clearly drawn. The governing board functions as an oversight body; it is not involved in the organization's day-to-day operations, which are handled by line management in individual business units and functional areas. The board is interested in results not the means by which those results are achieved.

The executive-centered governance model presupposes strong executive leadership, which should not be confused with executive sponsorship. An executive sponsor provides a critical link between information governance and organizational governance. An information governance program must have high-level sponsorship, preferably by an organizational executive—a so-called C-suite officer—who reports directly to the chief executive officer. The executive sponsor will communicate with other top officials to create awareness about the program's objectives, advocate for funding, help to eliminate barriers to program initiatives, and resolve problems that require executive intervention. All commentators agree that executive commitment is a critical success factor for governance initiatives.

An information governance program needs an engaged executive sponsor who recognizes the strategic value of information, understands an organization's information-related activities and issues, and has a vested business interest in the program's success. The executive sponsor may be an organizational official with information-related responsibilities. An organization's chief information officer (CIO), where present, is often cited as a good choice for an executive sponsor. Other C-suite executives with a strong interest in information-related matters include the general counsel or other chief legal officer (CLO), chief compliance officer (CCO), chief risk officer (CRO), chief security officer (CSO), chief privacy officer (CPO), chief knowledge officer (CKO), and chief administrative officer (CAO).

An information governance program's executive sponsor focuses on awareness and advocacy; the executive officer actually runs the program. With executive-centered information governance, an organization's executive officer works with the governing board to:

1. Identify strategic objectives and priorities,

2. Authorize specific information governance initiatives based on those objectives and priorities,

3. Obtain and allocate budgetary resources for information governance investments,

4. Define the information governance responsibilities of specific business units and functional areas, and

5. Ensure that stakeholders understand the information governance initiatives and activities for which they are responsible.

The executive officer may be a CIO or another high-level official who also serves as the program's executive sponsor. To provide the required leadership, some consultants, industry analysts, and others have suggested the creation of a new C-suite position, a chief information governance officer (CIGO), who would have enterprise-wide responsibility for an organization's information strategy, resources, and initiatives. Whether such a position would replace, complement, or report to an organization's CIO is not clear.

Policy Governance Model

The policy governance model, also known as the *Carver® model*, was introduced in the 1970s by John Carver, a specialist in organizational governance. Updated and refined since that time, the policy governance model has been widely adopted by companies, government agencies, and nongovernmental organizations in many countries. Its continued development is promoted by the International Policy Governance Association (IPGA), a not-for-profit organization for practitioners and consultants who use the model.

As its principal characteristic, the policy governance model maintains a sharply drawn distinction between governance and management:

• A governing board acts as "the informed voice and agent" of an organization's "owners," who may be the shareholders of a company, the public served by a government agency, or the community served by a not-for-profit organization.

• The policy governance model does not specify the size, composition, or structure of the governing board. It focuses on the board's purpose, which is to develop policies that articulate an organization's vision and objectives. Board members may be selected by an executive officer, other board members, stakeholder units, or others.

- The organization's management is responsible for implementing those policies without further direction from the board, which only becomes involved with management matters if board policies are violated. The governing board is not an advisory committee for operational matters.

The board focuses on an organization's mission and strategic priorities, which the policy governance model characterizes as "ends." Management is responsible for the "means," which must be compatible with board policies. If an information governance board issues a policy that mandates the replacement of in-house computer operations by cloud-based services, for example, management in the information technology unit is responsible for implementing the policy. If an information governance board issues a policy that mandates an organizational transition from paper to electronic media for retention of official copies, management in the records management unit is responsible for implementing the policy. If the governing board issues a policy that mandates specific responses to data breaches, the information security or legal department is responsible for implementing the policy.

The policy governance model is designed to empower management not interfere with it. The distinction between ends and means is critical. Board policies specify what is to be done. They do not replace management-level policies and procedures that specify how it will be done. In an information governance program, a policy governance board monitors organizational performance with respect to board policies, but it is not otherwise involved in information-related operations. The governing board focuses on outcomes rather than the means to achieve those outcomes.

The policy governance model is compatible with strong programmatic management by a CIO, CIGO, or other executive officer, but—unlike the executive-driven governance model—the executive officer is not a board member and does not direct the board's deliberations. With its focus on vision and objectives, the policy governance model can also work in a nonhierarchical setting where management responsibilities are decentralized at the stakeholder level.

The policy governance model can coexist with subordinate or related governance initiatives that may adopt different governance models. An organization may adopt the policy governance model for its information governance program, for example, and the executive-centered model for data governance, IT governance, or other governance initiatives discussed later in this part.

The policy governance model is well suited to organizations that are reasonably satisfied with their existing information-related business functions and established information management practices but desire to ensure strategic alignment of information-related initiatives with organizational priorities. The policy governance model requires little or no change in organizational structure, but board policies may ultimately require significant changes in organizational behavior.

Collaborative Governance Model

As its name implies, the collaborative governance model emphasizes cooperation and consensus. A collaborative governance board's membership is drawn from an organization's business units and other stakeholders. The board's composition may be rigidly prescribed to ensure that major stakeholders are represented. In the case of information governance, board members represent business units and functional areas that are directly involved with or deeply affected by the organization's information-related strategies, policies, decisions, and initiatives. Board members are typically department heads or high-level departmental employees who report directly to top management in their respective business units or functional areas.

Depending on the organization, a collaborative governing board may:

- Develop information-related strategies, objectives, and priorities.

- Define enterprise-wide standards and policies for information-related initiatives.

- Review and approve information-related projects and practices that impact multiple business units or functional areas. (Individual business units and functional areas are responsible for projects and practices that relate exclusively to their own operations.)

- Review information-related projects and practices for compliance with legal requirements and internal policies.

- Advise top management about the significance and potential consequences of legal and regulatory changes or other developments that may affect the organization's information-related initiatives and activities.

- Review and approve information-related expenditures that exceed a predefined threshold.

- Request, receive, and review reports about the status of specific information-related matters.

- Authorize needs assessments, gap analyses, impact assessments, compliance audits, or other evaluations of information-related initiatives or activities.

The collaborative governance model is nonhierarchical. The governing board needs a chairperson or convener, but the collaborative model does not presuppose the existence of a CIO, CIGO, or other strong executive leader to whom the board will report. Governing authority and accountability are decentralized among board members who are collectively empowered to make decisions, which reflect a consensus of stakeholders' perspectives. The collaborative governance model is well-suited to organizational cultures that emphasize negotiation and consensus-building as decision-making processes.

With the collaborative governance model, information governance is less of a formally established program than an agreed-upon concept. By participating as members, stakeholders accept the need for enterprise-wide information governance and acknowledge the collaborative board's authority over their business units and functional areas. Stakeholder units retain control over their own operations, but the governing board's decisions may have a significant impact on operations. Communication, interaction, and compromise are essential to deal with conflicts of interest and disputes among stakeholders, which are inevitable in any group that represents multiple viewpoints and business functions. In its deliberations and actions, the board must balance the best interests of the organization against the preferences of individual stakeholders. The board's goal is to reach agreement, but not necessarily unanimity, among members.

Working Board Model

As its name suggests, a working board is actively involved in an organization's operational and administrative activities, possibly including direct supervision of line management and staff in individual business units and functional areas:

- As its defining characteristic, the working board model does not draw a clear distinction between governance and management.

- Board members are typically the heads or representatives of stakeholder units. A strong executive is not required. The working board functions as an executive body rather than a true governing body. It sets its own agenda and strategic direction.

- A working board may have hands-on involvement with detailed aspects of program operation. In an information governance context, for example, a working board may be involved in the development of records retention schedules, the destruction of records with elapsed retention periods, or the selection of enterprise content management software, email archiving systems, cloud-based information providers, consultants, or other information management products and services.

As an obvious problem, a working board's activities may verge on micromanagement as the board may assume duties that are normally exercised by an organization's line management and staff. The working board model is rarely workable in organizations with well-established business units or functional areas. It is best for small organizations or for supporting new initiatives that will later transition to a different governance model.

Advisory Board Model

In this governance model, a board provides advice to an organization's management about information-related matters. An advisory board governs in a nominal sense only. It is more accurately characterized as an advisory committee:

- Unlike a true governing board, an advisory board does not have the authority to make decisions or to set policy. Its role is limited to assistance and support. An advisory board is not involved in operations.

- Advisory board members are selected for their backgrounds, influence, and contacts. Board members are selected by an executive officer, possibly based on recommendations of knowledgeable persons. The executive officer defines the advisory board's agenda.

- As with the collaborative governance model, board members represent major stakeholders but, unlike a collaborative governing body, an advisory board may contain external members—consultants, college professors, employees of comparable organizations, or others—who are selected for their subject expertise or experience.

This governance model may be suitable for an information governance program where strong executive leadership wants informed, nonbinding guidance about information-related policies, decisions, initiatives, or other matters.

A comparison of the governance models presented in this section is shown in Table 1 in Appendix A.

Stakeholder Roles and Responsibilities

An information governance stakeholder is a business unit or functional area that is involved with or affected by an organization's information-related strategies, policies, or processes.

Virtually all organizational units and functional areas are involved with and affected by information, but the principal stakeholders in an information governance program are directly responsible for information-related operations or information-dependent activities.

The following sections define and discuss the roles and responsibilities of key information governance stakeholders: records management, information technology, information security, risk management, compliance, legal affairs, data science, and archival administration.[24] The relative importance of these stakeholders varies among organizations, but they collectively address the core issues and concerns of information governance: (1) managing the information lifecycle, (2) making information accessible and usable, (3) safeguarding information assets, (4) ensuring compliance with information-related legal and regulatory requirements, and (5) addressing information-related risks.

Records Management

As defined in ISO 15489-1, *Information and Documentation—Records Management—Part 1: General*, records

The relationship between an information governance program and stakeholder units is based on the difference between governance and management. Information governance defines an organization's information-related objectives and develops high-level strategies, policies, and processes to support those objectives. Stakeholders are responsible for implementing those strategies, policies, and processes in the context of specific information-related operations and delegated authority, subject to evaluation and oversight by information governance. Information governance complements and coexists with existing stakeholder functions that have managerial responsibility for specific information-related processes, activities, and operations. Information governance establishes the strategic direction and policy guidance for stakeholder functions. It does not replace them or diminish their importance.

---

[24] This list of information governance stakeholders is not comprehensive. In some organizations, other stakeholders—information-dependent business units, such as a finance or tax department, for example, or an organization's library, which maintains technical or business information for research purposes—might be included.

management is responsible for "the efficient and systematic control" of records that are "created, received, and maintained as evidence and information by an organization or person, in pursuance of legal obligations or in the transaction of business." Records management is a well-established staff function and a key stakeholder in any information governance initiative. The records management function deals, to a greater or lesser extent, with creation, collection, storage, use, analysis, distribution, disclosure, retention, disposition, and protection of information in all formats, in all parts of an organization, and in all locations where an organization operates.

Although some of its information-related activities are also performed by other organizational units, records management's role as an information governance stakeholder focuses on lifecycle management of recorded information in electronic and physical formats. Among its responsibilities, records management:

1. Develops policies, rules, and guidelines that specify how long computer data, paper documents, photographs, video recordings, audio recordings, and other information-bearing objects must be kept to satisfy an organization's legal, regulatory, fiscal, and operational requirements.

2. Develops policies and standards for retention of information in specific formats, on specific media, or in specific locations.

3. Develops policies and business processes for defensible destruction of obsolete information in the regular course of an organization's business in full compliance with applicable laws and regulations.

4. Develops and implements guidelines and business processes for efficient, cost-effective management of inactive information that warrants continued retention.

5. Evaluates and recommends technologies and business processes for organization and retrieval of information.

6. Develops and implements backup protection and disaster recovery plans for physical (paper and photographic) records that support mission-critical operations.

Information Technology

Information technology (IT) is the generic name for the business function that develops and maintains an organization's computing and networking infrastructure, including computer and communications hardware, software, and networking components and services. The information technology function may be centralized, decentralized, or both, with some computing and networking resources consolidated at the enterprise level and others managed by individual business units or contracted to external providers. Whether operated in-house or outsourced, information technology deals exclusively with digital information. Paper documents and photographic records, which are important information resources in many organizations, are outside its scope.

As an information governance stakeholder, the information technology function plays an enabling role. It provides the technological resources, expertise, and support required to implement information governance strategies and policies issued by a governing board or other stakeholders. Specifically, information technology has the following responsibilities:

1. Evaluate, acquire, implement, and manage computing and networking components and services for input, storage, retrieval, distribution, and protection of digital information.

2. Optimize the utilization of technological resources for efficient, cost-effective storage and processing of digital information.

3. Implement and manage technologies and processes to ensure the continued accessibility and reliability of digital information throughout its lifecycle.

4. Implement controls to prevent unauthorized access to digital information.

5. Implement and manage processes to identify and delete obsolete digital information as defined by an organization's retention policies, while preventing deletion of information that must be preserved for legal proceedings.

6. Develop and implement backup protection and disaster recovery capability for digital information that supports mission-critical operations.

Information Security

ISO/IEC 27000, *Information technology—Security techniques—Information security management systems—Overview and vocabulary*, defines information security as the "preservation of confidentiality, integrity and availability of information." It also notes that information security may be concerned with the authenticity and reliability of information and with ensuring that business units and functional areas are held accountable for complying with security requirements for information in their custody or under their control.

The information security function prevents, protects against, and responds to data breaches, failures of control, and other events that involve unauthorized access, disclosure, improper use, alteration, or destruction of an organization's information. The information security function is particularly concerned with unauthorized disclosure of confidential information, such as business plans and financial data, and sensitive personal information, including personally identifiable information (PII), protected health information (PHI), and payment card information (PCI).

Depending on the organization, the information security function may be based in an information technology unit or in a security unit with broad responsibilities for safeguarding an organization's personnel and property. As an information governance stakeholder, information security works with business units, functional areas, and other stakeholders to:

1. Develop plans, policies, and processes to prevent unauthorized disclosure of information, unauthorized access to information, and other security lapses.

2. Respond to and investigate security events that involve an organization's information resources.

3. Evaluate and recommend equipment, software, and services to safeguard an organization's information resources.

4. Identify information resources that require special security arrangements.

5. Develop policies and processes for reliable, secure destruction of obsolete information resources, including storage devices and media that contain confidential or sensitive information.

Risk Management

ISO Guide 73, *Risk management—Vocabulary*, defines risk management as "coordinated activities to direct and control an organization with regard to risk," which is broadly defined as the "effect of uncertainty on objectives." ISO Guide 73 defines uncertainty as a deficiency of information, understanding, or knowledge related to the likelihood or consequences of an event. As discussed in ISO Guide 73, risk is often expressed as a combination of the adverse consequences of an event and the likelihood of occurrence of that event.

Uncertainty and risk are characteristics of all organizational initiatives, including information-related operations and activities. While all information governance stakeholders have risk-related responsibilities, many companies, government agencies, and nonprofit entities have a formally established risk management function headed by a chief risk officer or comparable high-level executive who has enterprise-wide authority and accountability for risk-related planning and decision making. In some organizations, risk management is integrated with compliance. That approach recognizes the importance of risks associated with an organization's failure to comply with legal and regulatory requirements, but enterprise risk management has a broader scope than compliance. It deals with the full range of strategic risks, which result from failed plans or decisions related to an organization's objectives, and operational risks, which result from inadequate internal processes or external circumstances. In some organizations, the risk management function is responsible for insurance and other risk transfer arrangements.

As it relates to information governance, risk may be associated with internal factors, such as an organization's information-related policies and practices, or external events, such as financial, regulatory, technological, geopolitical, or environmental developments, that can affect an organization's information-related objectives or operations. **Information assurance**, an aspect of risk management, is specifically concerned with strategic and operational risks associated with creation, collection, processing, storage, use, and distribution of information. Information assurance is closely aligned with but distinct from information security. The two disciplines have a complementary relationship. Both are concerned with accessibility, integrity, and reliability of information, but information assurance emphasizes identification and analysis of threats and vulnerabilities that place information assets at risk, while information security focuses on the implementation of tactics and technologies that protect information from unauthorized use, disclosure, modification, or destruction.

As an information governance stakeholder, risk management has the following responsibilities:

1. Identify, assess, and monitor internal risks associated with information-related strategies, policies, practices, initiatives, and operations.

2. Identify, evaluate, and monitor external events that threaten an organization's information resources.

3. Develop and communicate plans, policies, and processes to anticipate, mitigate, transfer, or eliminate information-related risks.

4. Direct, coordinate, and monitor an organization's responses to specific information-related risks.

Compliance

According to ISO 19600, *Compliance Management Systems—Guidelines*, **compliance** involves meeting an obligation or requirement, which is defined as a "need or expectation that is stated, generally implied, or obligatory." As a control function, the mission of compliance is to provide reasonable assurance that an organization conforms to applicable obligations and requirements, which may be developed internally or specified by external sources. Internal obligations are based on organizational policies, procedures, guidelines, and codes of conduct that mandate specific behavior. External sources that specify compliance requirements include laws, regulations, international standards, and industry norms.

Standalone compliance departments headed by a chief compliance officer (CCO) or a comparably high-level official are encountered in heavily regulated industries such as financial services, pharmaceuticals, healthcare, utilities, oil, telecommunications, and transportation. Such departments deal specifically and exclusively with compliance issues. In other organizations, compliance is a functional area within a legal affairs or risk management unit.

Compliance is often driven by legal and regulatory requirements, but it is also concerned with nonlegal matters. Compliance must address risks associated with violations of internal and external mandates, but—as described previously—risk management deals with a much broader range of issues. Compliance is sometimes associated and confused with internal audit, but the two functions have distinct missions and different approaches to accomplishing their objectives. Both functions have oversight responsibilities, but compliance works closely with individual organizational units to align their practices with internal and external mandates while internal audit must maintain its independence in order to determine whether compliance has actually been achieved.

Information-related practices are deeply affected by internal policies and by thousands of laws and regulations. As an information governance stakeholder, compliance works with business units, functional areas, and other stakeholders to:

1. Review information-related policies, procedures, and practices for alignment with compliance requirements.

2. Identify, monitor, and alert organizational units about legal and regulatory developments and trends that affect information-related initiatives and operations.

3. Monitor information-related initiatives and operations to determine whether and to what extent they comply with internal and external mandates.

4. Provide advice, assistance, and interpretations about compliance-related matters.

5. Conduct internal inquiries and investigations into possible compliance violations.

6. Assembles information for submissions to government agencies and other regulatory authorities.

7. Serve as a contact point for inquiries, reviews, investigations, and examinations by regulatory authorities.

Legal Affairs

Depending on the organization, the legal affairs function may be known as the *legal department*, *law department*, or *legal services department*. The department head is typically a high-level C-suite official—a chief legal officer, general counsel, or chief counsel. As an organization's legal advisor and authority, the legal affairs function drafts, reviews, and approves contracts, agreements, and other legal documents; prepares legal filings; deals with labor relations issues and personnel problems; interprets laws and regulations; handles intellectual property matters; initiates and responds to inquiries and complaints with legal implications; and provides legal opinions and advice about organizational strategies and operations.

Legal affairs units are also responsible for **discovery**—the investigative phase of litigation when opposing parties can obtain information to help them prepare for trial. Discovery involves the identification, collection, organization, indexing, review, and dissemination of information in electronic and physical formats. Depending on the circumstances, discovery may be handled in-house or by external counsel with or without the assistance of litigation support contractors.

As an information governance stakeholder, legal affairs works with business units, functional areas, and other stakeholders to:

1. Align information-related policies, procedures, and practices with the organization's legal obligations and requirements.

2. Provide opinions and interpretations about laws and regulations that deal with creation, collection, retention, use, distribution, disclosure, protection, and disposition of information.

3. Issue legal holds to preserve information deemed relevant for litigation, government investigations, or other legal proceedings.

4. Perform or coordinate information-related discovery for legal proceedings.

Data Science

Data science is an interdisciplinary field that employs a combination of statistics, mathematics, computer modeling, data visualization, pattern recognition, and machine learning to explore, extract, and analyze digital information. Data scientists typically work on specific questions that are generated by decision makers. A medical insurer, for example, may want to process claims data to identify excessive use of expensive diagnostic procedures by healthcare providers. A product designer may want to process order data to determine the impact of packaging characteristics on sales. A marketing manager may want to process Twitter messages in order to target advertising to specific groups. Data science is closely associated with large quantities of digital information, so-called big data, which is too voluminous to process by conventional means.

Some organizations have an enterprise-wide data science unit headed by a chief data scientist (CDS). That unit may be a standalone department or part of information technology. In other cases, business units add data scientists to their staffs or acquire data science capabilities from external providers when suitable problems arise. As an information governance stakeholder, data science is responsible for:

1. Defining policies and procedures for analyzing data, including issues related to privacy and data protection.

2. Identifying information needed for specific analytical projects and activities.

3. Collecting information from existing data sets and converting it to a format suitable for analysis or other use.

Archival Administration

The stakeholders described previously are principally concerned with information that supports an organization's business initiatives and operations. Archival administration, by contrast, deals with information that is no longer needed for business purposes but that has continuing value for cultural or scholarly research purposes. Such information is termed "archival," a description that reflects both its significance and its age. Archival administration is typically involved with the end stage of the information lifecycle. Archival information is often characterized as "historical," but historians are just one group of researchers that utilize archival records. Others include social scientists, political scientists, public policy analysts, urban planners, educators, journalists, economists, literary scholars, filmmakers, and genealogists.

Archival programs are well established in national and local government, where they are often required by law, and in many not-for-profit organizations, including universities, medical centers, professional societies, charities, foundations, religious groups, and cultural institutions. Some for-profit entities have established archives to preserve historical information about their founders, business operations, innovations, brands, products, and services. In addition to its scholarly value, information maintained by these archives may be useful for public relations, advertising, trademark protection, anniversary celebrations, investor relations, and other business purposes.

As an information governance stakeholder, archival administration is responsible for:

1. Identifying information with continuing value for historical, cultural, scholarly, or research purposes.

2. Developing policies and standards for permanent preservation of archival information in specific formats, on specific media, or in specific locations.

3. Evaluating and implementing technologies and business processes for organization, indexing, retrieval, protection, and long-term usability of archival information.

Stakeholder Interaction

Communal pursuit of organizational interests is a principal characteristic of governance initiatives. A siloed approach, in which stakeholders operate independently and—in some cases—competitively, is not compatible with effective governance.

Information governance must promote interaction, cooperation, and consultation among stakeholders. In the absence of communication and coordination, a given stakeholder may implement policies, make decisions, or take actions that adversely affect other stakeholders. An action that improves the efficiency or effectiveness of one information-related operation can have unintended consequences elsewhere in an organization. To maintain efficient operation of its email servers, for example, an organization's information technology unit may routinely delete messages that are more than six months old, but the potential destruction of messages with evidentiary value poses problems for litigation support and regulatory compliance. Similarly, a marketing department may want multidecade retention for customer order information, but long retention of personal information about customers can pose problems for information security and may violate national data protection laws.

While individual stakeholders understandably focus on their own responsibilities and operations, information governance takes a broader view. An information governance program must assess the organizational impact of local actions and balance the competing agendas of individual stakeholders to achieve results that are in the common interest. It must encourage dialogue, synergies, and consensus-building to identify potential problems, minimize disagreements among stakeholders, and resolve conflicts. The following sections discuss stakeholder involvement and interaction for specific information governance activities and business processes. The discussion is summarized in a responsibility assignment matrix—a so-called RACI chart—that identifies:

1. The stakeholder unit that is responsible (R) for doing the work associated with an activity or business process.

2. The stakeholder unit that is ultimately accountable (A) for correct completion and approval of the activity or business process.

3. The stakeholder units that must be consulted (C) for information or advice about the activity or business process.

4. The stakeholder units that are to be kept informed (I) but not formally consulted about the activity or business process.

In the RACI chart, the responsible and accountable stakeholders for a given activity or business process are identical but, within a given stakeholder unit, different employees may be responsible for doing the work and accountable for its correct completion. In an information technology unit, for example, systems analysts or technology planners may be responsible for evaluating and acquiring specific computing or networking services, but the CIO or other unit head is accountable for correct completion of that task. Similarly, staff attorneys in a legal affairs unit may issue holds to suspend destruction of information deemed relevant for litigation, but the general counsel or a comparable legal official must ensure that the holds were correctly issued. If an organization has appointed a CIGO or designated another high-level official to head its information governance program, that person may be accountable for many or all listed activities and business processes.

Records Management

With its enterprise-wide scope, records management affects and is affected by the responsibilities, interests, and activities of other information governance stakeholders. As the responsibility assignment matrix in Table 2 in Appendix B indicates, records management consults with and informs other stakeholders about specific activities and business processes for which it is accountable and responsible:

- **Interaction with information technology.** Records management consults with information technology to identify technological issues and concerns related to specific retention rules, storage formats and media, and disposition processes. In many organizations, electronic data is stored on servers that are operated or supervised by the information technology function. Although information technology does not specify retention rules for such data, it is responsible for implementing those retention rules, which may require software modifications or other procedural changes to identify data with elapsed retention periods. Records management also works with information technology to evaluate and select **enterprise content management** systems, records management application software, email archiving systems, and other technologies for organization, retrieval, and lifecycle management of recorded information. Information technology is not involved with management, protection, or disaster recovery issues related to physical records. A **records management application** is software that creates and maintains a reliable repository for retention of digital documents and other digital content. As explained next, information technology has principal disaster recovery responsibility for an organization's electronic information.

- **Interaction with information security.** Records management consults with information security to determine whether specific records retention rules pose security problems. Assuming that legal and operational requirements are satisfied, the information security function typically favors short retention periods; the longer information is kept, the greater the opportunity for unauthorized access, unauthorized disclosure, theft, or other security breaches. A security breach is a particular concern with confidential or sensitive information. Records management must consult with information security to develop policies and processes for defensible disposition of obsolete information. As discussed next, information security is responsible for developing policies and processes for obsolete information that requires secure destruction. Records management must consult with information security about protection and disaster recovery plans for mission-critical physical records. Information security may also be involved in the evaluation and approval of storage locations for physical records. Information security is not directly involved with the evaluation of technologies or the development of processes for organization and retrieval of information.

- **Interaction with risk management.** Records management consults with risk management to determine the impact of records retention policies on an organization's risk profile. Like the information security function, risk management is concerned about the potential impact of long retention periods on security breaches. In this context, risk management is concerned with analysis and evaluation of security risks associated with long retention, while information security is responsible for protecting information until its retention periods elapse. Risk management must also consider other retention-related issues and concerns. Long retention periods, for example, can increase the logistic burdens and costs of legal discovery, a consideration that is also important for legal affairs. On the other hand, risk management must assess the consequences of not having information that may be useful for operational reasons. Risk management is also concerned with retention formats and standards, which can affect the future usability of information; with storage locations for inactive records, which may pose problems of security and accessibility; with defensible destruction policies, which reduce an organization's exposure to fines and penalties; and with disaster recovery plans for mission-critical physical records. Risk management is not directly involved with the evaluation of technologies or the development of processes for organization and retrieval of information, but it may need to be informed about those matters.

- **Interaction with compliance.** Records management consults with compliance to identify internal and external mandates that affect or may be affected by information lifecycle policies and rules. While records and information managers perform legal research to identify recordkeeping requirements, the compliance function has the subject expertise to clarify and interpret laws and regulations that deal with records retention periods, the acceptability of specific storage formats and media, and disaster recovery requirements, as well as in-country retention requirements, limitations on cross-border information transfer, and other restrictions on the locations where information is stored. The compliance function can also contact regulatory authorities for opinions about or approval of an organization's records retention practices. Compliance is not directly involved with the evaluation of technologies or the development of processes for organization and retrieval of information, but it may need to be informed about those matters.

- **Interaction with legal affairs.** Records management has a long-standing relationship with the legal affairs function, which it routinely consults for advice and opinions about the legal acceptability of records retention and disposition policies, interpretations of recordkeeping laws and regulations, and contractual issues related to specific records management services such as offsite storage of records by commercial providers. In some organizations records management reports to the legal affairs function, which has final approval authority over records management policies and records retention schedules. Unless legal, regulatory, or contractual considerations apply, the legal affairs function is seldom involved in decisions about the management and protection of physical records or with recommendations about technologies for organization and retrieval of information (unless they directly relate to its own recordkeeping practices), but it may need to be informed about those matters.

- **Interaction with data science.** Records management consults with data science, to determine analytical requirements for retention of specific information. Data science projects may involve information that has no continuing legal or transactional value but that remains useful for analytical purposes. Unlike information security and risk management, data science typically favors long retention periods to ensure that information will be available when needed. Data science may also be affected by policies and practices that deal with data storage formats and media as well as technologies and processes for organization and retrieval of information. Data science is not involved with disposition policies for obsolete information. Because it deals exclusively with digital information, data science is not involved with any matters related to physical records.

- **Interaction with archival administration.** Records management consults with archival administration to ensure the preservation of information that has historical or scholarly value, as discussed in subsequent sections in this part. In some organizations, archival administration reviews retention schedules and policies that specify storage formats and media, but its concerns are limited to information of permanent value. Records management may consult archival administration to determine organization and retrieval requirements for permanent records, but those matters are often handled after the records are transferred to archival custody. Archival administration is not involved with defensible disposition of obsolete information, which is by definition nonarchival. Records management may need to inform archival administration about handling of inactive physical records and disaster recovery plans for physical records, but its interest is limited to their impact on archival records.

Information Technology

Information technology has an impact on all information governance initiatives and activities that involve electronic information. The responsibility assignment matrix in Table 2 in Appendix B shows that information technology consults with and informs other information governance stakeholders about decisions, initiatives, business processes, and other matters related to implementation and use of an organization's technological resources:

- **Interaction with records management.** Information technology consults with records management about implementation and utilization of computing and networking components and services that have an impact on lifecycle management of recorded information. These components and services include technologies and processes for storage, accessibility, and reliability of digital data. Information technology is responsible for disposition of digital data with elapsed retention periods, which are determined by records management. Records management and information technology must work together to ensure that this disposition is done. Records management is not directly involved with the implementation of controls and processes to prevent unauthorized access or provide protection for digital data, but it may need to be informed about those matters.

- **Interaction with information security.** Because many security issues relate to computing and networking operations, the information technology and information security functions must interact frequently and cooperate closely. In some organizations, as explained next, the information security function is based in an information technology unit. Even if it is not, information technology must consult with information security about implementation and utilization of computing and networking components and services that have security implications. Information security develops policies about access to and destruction of digital data. Information technology must implement those policies. Information technology must also consult with information security about protection and disaster recovery plans for digital data. Information security is not directly involved with the implementation of technologies and processes for continued accessibility and reliability of digital data or with optimal utilization of technological resources, but it may need to be informed about those matters.

- **Interaction with risk management.** Information technologies and processes can affect an organization's risk profile. Risk is mitigated or eliminated by technologies and processes that ensure continued accessibility and reliability of digital information, that prevent unauthorized access to digital information, that identify and delete obsolete digital information, and that provide disaster recovery capabilities for mission-critical digital information. Risk management can define expectations and provide useful advice about these information technology responsibilities. Information technology must consult with risk management about the acceptability of computing and networking components or services—cloud-based services or the attachment of personally owned devices to an organization's network, for example—that may pose threats or introduce vulnerabilities to which the organization was not previously exposed. In most organizations, risk management is not involved with initiatives that optimize the utilization of technological resources.

- **Interaction with compliance.** Information technology must consult with the compliance function to ensure that an organization's technological initiatives are compatible with internal and external mandates. Given the importance of digital information for audits, investigations, and regulatory submissions, information technology's responsibilities have a direct impact on an organization's ability to satisfy compliance requirements. Information technology's responsibilities also impact technologies and processes for continued accessibility and reliability of digital information, controls to prevent unauthorized access to digital information, processes to identify and delete obsolete digital information, and backup protection and disaster recovery initiatives. In certain industries, such as banking and pharmaceuticals, an organization's information technology operations may be subject to inspection by regulatory authorities. Consequently, the compliance function must be consulted about the acquisition or implementation of computing and networking components or services that may compromise compliance—the decision to use an out-of-country cloud-based service, for example, to store information that must be retained in the country. In most organizations, the compliance function is not involved with initiatives that optimize the utilization of technological resources.

- **Interaction with legal affairs.** Information technology must consult with legal affairs about the legal acceptability of controls to prevent unauthorized access to digital information, processes to identify and destroy obsolete digital information, and disaster recovery capabilities for mission-critical digital information. In most organizations, legal affairs must be consulted for contractual matters related to procurement of computing and networking components and services. Legal affairs needs to be informed about technologies and processes that ensure continued accessibility and reliability of digital information, but it does not provide advice or opinions that affect the implementation of those technologies and processes. In most organizations, the legal affairs function is not involved with initiatives that optimize the utilization of technological resources.

- **Interaction with data science.** Information technology must consult with the data science function to ensure that its analytical requirements are included in the planning process for acquisition and implementation of computing and networking components and services. In most organizations, the data science function does not provide direct input about other information technology responsibilities, but it may need to be informed about them. As discussed later in this part, the data science function may be based in an information technology unit. Where that is the case, information technology's responsibilities and data science interests are closely aligned.

- **Interaction with archival administration.** Information technology must consult with archival administration to ensure that the computing and networking infrastructure is compatible with permanent preservation of digital information of archival value. Archival administration is also concerned about information technology initiatives related to optimal utilization of storage resources and continued accessibility and reliability of digital information. Archival administration is not consulted for advice and assistance about other information technology responsibilities, but it may need to be informed about them.

Information Security

Like records management and information technology, information security has an impact on all information governance activities. The information security function must work with other stakeholders to fulfill its responsibilities:

- **Interaction with records management.** Information security must consult with records management when developing policies and processes for secure destruction of obsolete information, an important lifecycle issue that has a direct impact on records management initiatives. To identify information that requires special security arrangements, the information security function may need to draw on records management's knowledge of departmental recordkeeping practices and requirements. Records management does not provide direct input about other information security responsibilities, but it needs to be informed about them.

- **Interaction with information technology.** All information security responsibilities have an impact on information technology initiatives and operations. The information security function develops policies and processes to prevent security lapses and ensure that obsolete information is destroyed in a secure manner. The information technology function must implement those policies and processes for digital information in its custody or under its supervisory control. Information security must consult with information technology to ensure that an organization's computing and networking components and services are compatible with security requirements. Information security must also consult with information technology to fulfill its responsibilities for investigating security events and identifying special security requirements for digital information.

- **Interaction with risk management.** Information security must work closely with risk management, which also deals with information-related threats and vulnerabilities. Risk management can provide valuable input for development of policies and processes to prevent security lapses and ensure secure destruction of obsolete information. Risk management must also be consulted for investigation of security events, to help identify information that requires special security arrangements, and for advice or opinions about equipment, software, and services to protect information.

- **Interaction with compliance.** Information security must consult with the compliance function when developing policies to prevent security lapses or when investigating data breaches and other events that may violate laws and regulations. Security incidents related to data protection and personal privacy are widely cited examples. Information security must also consult with the compliance function to identify information that requires special security arrangements, for clarification or interpretation of regulatory requirements for secure destruction of obsolete information, and for advice or opinions about equipment, software, and services to protect information that is subject to internal or external compliance mandates.

- **Interaction with legal affairs.** Most information security responsibilities have legal implications. Information security must consult with the legal function for advice and opinions about policies to prevent security lapses and to ensure secure destruction of obsolete information. Legal affairs must also be involved in investigations of security events that involve information resources, especially where unauthorized access, unauthorized disclosure, or other security breaches involve confidential information or violate laws or regulations. Legal affairs may be consulted about information resources that require special security arrangements. Unless contractual issues are involved, the legal affairs function is seldom involved in the evaluation of equipment, software, or services to protect information.

- **Interaction with data science.** Information security needs to inform the data science function about policies related to security lapses and secure destruction of obsolete information. Data science rarely provides direct input to those policies, but it is responsible for complying with them for digital information involved in its analytical projects. Data science may work on projects that involve personally identifiable information, protected health information, or other sensitive information. Information security must consult with data science to identify projects that require special security arrangements. Data science is not directly involved with evaluation and selection of computing and networking components and services to protect information, but it may need to be informed about such components and services.

- **Interaction with archival administration.** Information security must consult with archival administration to identify archival information with special security requirements. Archival administration is not directly involved in other information security responsibilities, but it may need to be informed about those matters.

Risk Management

As previously noted, risk is a component of all information-related initiatives and activities. The risk management function must work with other information governance stakeholders to fulfill its responsibilities:

- **Interaction with records management.** Records management can provide risk management with useful advice about external threats and internal vulnerabilities that can destroy mission-critical information or render it unusable. Risk management must consult with records management to develop policies, plans, and processes that anticipate, mitigate, eliminate, and monitor responses to risks associated with lifecycle management policies and records retention, which is the focus of records management's information governance responsibilities. Records management is responsible for implementing risk management plans and processes for mission-critical physical records.

- **Interaction with information technology.** Risk management must consult with information technology for advice and assistance in identifying and evaluating threats and vulnerabilities associated with an organization's technological infrastructure and the digital information it processes, stores, and makes available. Drawing on its expertise and experience, information technology can provide useful advice about system failures, malicious software, data corruption, network intrusions, and other risks associated with specific computing and networking components and services. Risk management must consult with information technology to develop plans and processes that anticipate, mitigate, eliminate, and monitor responses to threats and vulnerabilities that affect digital information. Information technology is responsible for implementing risk management plans and processes for digital information in its custody or under its supervisory control.

- **Interaction with information security.** As previously noted, risk management and information security responsibilities are closely aligned. Risk management must consult with information security about plans, policies, and processes that anticipate, mitigate, eliminate, and monitor risks related to theft, loss, disclosure, or corruption of information.

- **Interaction with compliance.** Risk management must consult with the compliance function to identify threats and vulnerabilities associated with internal or external mandates. The compliance function has the expertise and experience to advise risk management about the likelihood and consequences of audit deficiencies, regulatory violations, and other compliance failures associated with incomplete recordkeeping, improper information disclosure, inadequate data protection, or other information-related problems. The compliance function can advise risk management about plans and processes to anticipate, mitigate, eliminate, and monitor responses to information-related risks associated with compliance mandates.

- **Interaction with legal affairs.** Many information-related risks have legal implications or consequences. Risk management must consult with legal affairs for clarifications, interpretations, and opinions related to its information governance responsibilities. Legal affairs can help risk management identify information-related risks associated with civil litigation, contracts, shareholder agreements, government investigations, insurance coverage, labor disputes, patent infringements, copyright and trademark violations, and other legal matters. The legal affairs function can advise risk management about plans and processes to anticipate, mitigate, transfer, eliminate, and monitor information-related risks that involve legal exposure.

- **Interaction with data science.** Legal and compliance risks are associated with data science projects that involve personally identifiable information, protected health information, or other sensitive information. Risk management needs to inform data science about risks associated with specific analytical projects and activities, and it must consult with data science to develop plans and processes to anticipate, mitigate, or eliminate such risks.

- **Interaction with archival administration.** As previously defined, archival administration is responsible for permanent preservation of information assets of continuing value. Archival administration can provide risk management with useful advice about external threats and internal vulnerabilities that can destroy archival information or render it unusable. Risk management must consult with archival administration to develop plans and processes that anticipate, mitigate, eliminate, and monitor responses to such risks.

Compliance

The compliance function must work with other information governance stakeholders to fulfill its responsibilities:

- **Interaction with records management.** Compliance must consult with records management to align lifecycle management policies and retention guidance with internal and external mandates. Compliance works with records management to identify recordkeeping requirements in laws and regulations. When preparing retention guidance, records management typically conducts legal research to identify such requirements, but compliance can clarify, interpret, and advise about laws and regulations that impact retention policies and practices. Compliance consults with records management when investigating recordkeeping practices that may violate internal or external mandates—a department's failure to comply with the organization's retention schedule or with regulatory requirements for information in its custody, for example. Compliance may also seek records management's help when assembling information for submission to regulatory authorities.

- **Interaction with information technology.** Compliance must consult with information technology to ensure that computing and networking resources and services are consistent with internal and external mandates. Compliance also consults with information technology when investigating possible violations of internal or external mandates that involve digital information or when assembling information from digital sources for submission to regulatory authorities. Information technology is not directly involved with the compliance function's other responsibilities, but it may need to be informed about them.

- **Interaction with information security.** The compliance function must consult with information security to align an organization's security policies and practices with internal and external mandates. Compliance also works with information security when monitoring activities or investigating possible violations that involve security matters. Information security is not directly involved with the compliance function's other responsibilities, but it may need to be informed about them.

- **Interaction with risk management.** As previously discussed, the compliance and risk management functions have closely aligned responsibilities. In organizations that do not have a formally established compliance unit, compliance is typically a risk management responsibility. Compliance must consult with risk management when reviewing and monitoring an organization's policies and practices to ensure consistency with internal and external mandates. It must also consult with risk management when investigating possible compliance violations. The compliance function identifies the violations; risk management assesses their impact. Compliance must inform risk management about legal and regulatory developments, clarifications, interpretations, inquiries, or interactions with regulatory authorities that may impact the organization's risk profile. Risk management is not directly involved with the submission of information to regulatory authorities, but it may need to be informed about such submissions.

- **Interaction with legal affairs.** Compliance must work closely with legal affairs to fulfill its information governance responsibilities. Compliance must consult with legal affairs for advice, clarifications, interpretations, and opinions about legal aspects of internal and external mandates that deal with information-related policies, processes, initiatives, and activities. Legal affairs must also be consulted about inquiries and investigations into possible compliance violations as well as submissions, inquiries, and other interactions with regulatory authorities.

- **Interaction with data science.** Data science projects may be affected by internal and external mandates related to collection, storage, use, and dissemination of information. Data science projects may deal with personally identifiable information, protected health information, or other confidential information that is covered by an organization's internal codes of conduct and by data protection laws and other regulatory requirements. In some circumstances, a data science project may require approval by an institutional review board. The compliance function must confirm that approval has been obtained before a project begins. In some countries, laws require that personal information be rendered anonymous before it is made available for data science projects. The compliance function must inform data science about internal and external mandates that apply to its analytical projects.

- **Interaction with archival administration.** Archival administration may maintain information that is subject to compliance mandates. Archival records may contain personally identifiable information, protected health information, or other confidential information of interest to historians, genealogists, and other researchers. Although archival records do not deal with current matters, they are still subject to internal codes of conduct and government regulations that protect sensitive information. The compliance function must consult with archival administration to ensure that policies and processes for access to such information are compatible with internal and external mandates. Archival administration must be informed about compliance requirements that apply to its initiatives and activities.

Legal Affairs

The legal affairs function has broad responsibilities that have a direct or indirect impact on all information governance activities. Legal affairs must interact with other stakeholders to fulfill its responsibilities:

- **Interaction with records management.** Legal affairs must consult with records management to align lifecycle management policies and retention guidance with legal requirements. In some organizations, the legal affairs function has approval authority over records management policies and retention guidelines. At a minimum, it reviews the organization's retention policies and schedule for legal acceptability. When preparing information-related opinions and interpretations, legal affairs may seek input from records management. The legal affairs function consults with records management when issuing legal holds or preparing for discovery proceedings to identify the organizational units that have relevant records in their custody or under their supervisory control. Legal affairs also collaborates with records management to ensure that legal holds are understood and observed by organizational units.

- **Interaction with information technology.** Legal affairs must consult with information technology for legal review of policies and contracts related to procurement and implementation of technology components and services. When preparing opinions or interpretations about information-related matters, legal affairs may seek input from information technology. The legal affairs function must also consult with information technology when issuing legal holds or preparing for discovery proceedings that involve digital information.

- **Interaction with information security.** Legal affairs must consult with the information security function to align an organization's security policies and practices with legal requirements. Legal affairs may consult with information security when preparing opinions or interpretations about policies or practices that have security implications. Information security is not directly involved with legal holds or discovery proceedings, but it may need to be informed about such matters.

- **Interaction with risk management.** The legal affairs function affects and is affected by an organization's information-related risk profile. Legal affairs must consult with risk management to ensure that risk-related policies and practices are legally acceptable and aligned with the organization's legal requirements. Legal affairs must consult with risk management when issuing legal holds or preparing for discovery for litigation, government investigation, or other legal proceedings.

- **Interaction with compliance.** Legal affairs must consult with the compliance function to ensure that internal mandates are aligned with the organization's legal requirements and that compliance policies and processes are consistent with legal and regulatory requirements. Legal affairs may consult the compliance function to discuss compliance with court orders or other requirements related to discovery proceedings and preservation of evidence.

- **Interaction with data science.** Legal affairs must consult with data science to ensure that policies and processes for collection, use, and distribution of information associated with analytical projects are legally acceptable and aligned with the organization's legal requirements. The data science function is not directly involved with preparation of legal holds, but it may be subject to them for information in its custody. The legal affairs function may consult with data science for advice and assistance with discovery matters for which analytical processes or software may be useful.

- **Interaction with archival administration.** Legal affairs must consult with archival administration to ensure that organizational policies and processes for access to and protection of archival information are aligned with legal requirements. Archival administration is not directly involved with preparation of legal holds or discovery proceedings, but it may be subject to them for information in its custody.

Data Science

Data science collaborates with other information governance stakeholders to fulfill its highly focused responsibilities:

- **Interaction with records management.** Data science must consult with records management to ensure its analytical requirements are addressed in retention policies and schedules. In some cases, information needed for analytical projects has no continuing legal or transactional value. If data science's requirements are not considered, the information might be destroyed.

- **Interaction with information technology.** Data science depends on information technology's ability to store and process large quantities of digital data. Data science must consult with information technology to ensure that technological resources and digital information are available for analytical projects. Data science must also consult with information technology for assistance with collecting and converting information from existing data sets.

- **Interaction with information security.** Data science projects may involve personally identifiable information, protected health information, and other confidential information that must be protected against unauthorized access, disclosure, or corruption during all phases of an analytical project. To prevent data breaches and other adverse events, data science must consult with information security to align its policies and processes with the organization's information security requirements.

- **Interaction with risk management.** Analytical projects that involve large quantities of confidential information can increase an organization's risk exposure. Data science must consult with the risk management function to identify, mitigate, and eliminate risks associated with specific analytical projects. In some organizations, data science may be required to submit project proposals to risk management for review and approval.

- **Interaction with compliance.** Data science must consult with compliance to confirm that policies and procedures for analytical projects are consistent with internal codes of conduct and external mandates, including data protection and privacy regulations. Data science must also inform compliance about analytical projects that involve personally identifiable information, protected health information, or other confidential information that is subject to internal codes of conduct or external restrictions on use or dissemination.

- **Interaction with legal affairs.** Data science must consult with legal affairs to review legal issues that apply to analytical projects. Such legal issues may relate to data science policies, analytical procedures, or the types of information associated with specific analytical projects.

- **Interaction with archival administration.** Data science projects may require analysis of historical information in the custody of archival administration. Data science must consult with archival administration to identify archival information that is relevant for specific analytical projects.

Archival Administration

Archival administration cooperates with other information governance stakeholders to fulfill its responsibilities:

- **Interaction with records management.** Archival administration and records management are related disciplines. In government and not-for-profit organizations, archival administration and records management are often combined in the same department. While both disciplines manage the lifecycle of recorded information, archival administration's involvement is limited to information of enduring value. Archival administration must consult with records management to ensure that archival value is considered when retention guidance is developed for specific types of information and that information of permanent value is identified in an organization's records retention schedule. Records management is not involved with the development of policies and standards for permanent preservation or the evaluation and implementation of technologies and processes for archival information, but it needs to be informed about those matters.

- **Interaction with information technology.** Archival administration must consult with information technology to determine storage locations and file formats for digital information of continuing value for historical and scholarly purposes. Archival administration must consult with information technology when developing policies and standards for permanent preservation of digital information. In some organizations, information technology is responsible for implementing those policies and standards, which must be compatible with its technological infrastructure and capabilities. Archival administration must consult with information technology about archival management or digital preservation applications that will be installed on servers operated by or under the supervisory control of information technology.

- **Interaction with information security.** Archival administration must consult with information security to confirm that technologies or processes for archival information are consistent with the organization's security requirements.

- **Interaction with risk management.** Archival administration must consult with risk management to ensure that its policies and practices, including processes and technologies for permanent preservation of information, do not increase the organization's risk profile. Risk management must be assured, for example, that permanent preservation of personally identifiable information, protected health information, or other confidential information will not expose an organization to violations of data protection and privacy laws. Such laws allow the retention of personal information for research purposes, but the information must be anonymized.

- **Interaction with compliance.** Archival administration must consult with the compliance function to ensure that permanent preservation of specific types of information does not violate laws or regulations that require the destruction of information after a specified period of time.

- **Interaction with legal affairs.** Archival administration must consult with the legal affairs function to obtain legal advice and opinions about the legal acceptability of its policies and practices related to specific types of archival information such as trade secrets, documents with copyrighted content, documents that were given to an organization in confidence, or other information that may be subject to legal restrictions on use or disclosure. Archival administration will also consult with legal affairs about contractual issues related to the acquisition and implementation of archives management software or services.

- **Interaction with data science.** Archival administration will inform data science about its policies, standards, technologies, and processes for permanent preservation of archival administration.

Related Governance Initiatives

Information governance must coexist and interact with other governance initiatives that deal with specific information-related matters or that have an impact on an organization's information-related policies and practices. Like information governance, these initiatives are focused extensions of corporate governance.

They have formally established governance frameworks that promote stakeholder cooperation and collaboration based on clearly defined roles and responsibilities, and they are subject to compliance requirements and risk management issues. Th following sections discuss the purpose and scope of these governance initiati and their relationship to information governance.

Data Governance

The *The DAMA Guide to the Data Management Body of Knowledge (DAMA-DMBOK)*—an authoritative guide issued by DAMA International, a not-for-profit association that deals with data resources and enterprise information management—defines **data governance** as "the exercise of authority, control, and shared decision making (planning, monitoring, and enforcement) over the management of data assets."[25] This definition is similar to definitions of information governance previously cited. Both fields emphasize the alignment of information-related initiatives with organizational objectives, but data governance has a narrower focus than information governance. It deals exclusively with digital information; paper and photographic records are out of scope. Some data governance initiatives are further limited to digital information contained in databases, data warehouses, and similar repositories. Unstructured content—digital documents, email messages, websites, social media content, audio recordings, and video recordings—is excluded.

Regardless of scope, data governance is concerned with the availability, usability, quality, integrity, security, protection, stewardship, and control of an organization's digital information. Information governance shares these concerns for information in all formats. Data governance initiatives are more focused: they typically target specific issues related to digital information such as improving the accessibility of data by an organization's authorized employees and business associates or ensuring that data is available to meet specific compliance requirements. Data governance is aligned with but separate from IT governance, which deals with technological resources for capture, storage, control, protection, and distribution of digital information. Data governance focuses on information not technology.

Data governance is closely associated with quality initiatives for mission-critical digital information. Master data governance, also known as *master data management (MDM)*, is variously considered a component of data governance or a separate but related initiative. As discussed in Part 3, master data management is concerned with creating and maintaining authoritative reference data—the core information needed to support an organization's initiatives and operations, including decision making, transaction processing, and regulatory submissions. Master data management initiatives typically focus on specific subject areas such as customer information, supplier information, personnel information, and product information. In the absence of master data management, this essential data may be scattered among multiple repositories, some of which may contain incorrect, incomplete, or out-of-date information. To create a master set of high-quality data, data governance develops policies, standards, and processes to consolidate, eliminate errors, remove redundancy and other extraneous content, and resolve inconsistencies in an organization's data. The resulting master data is an enterprise-wide collection of reliable, up-to-date information to be used by multiple processes and applications.

IT Governance

ISO/IEC 38500, *Information technology—Governance of IT for the organization*, ~~d~~ines **IT governance** as the "system by which the current and future use of IT is

---

5   *The DAMA Guide to the Data Management Body of Knowledge (DAMA-DMBOK)*. Bradley Beach, NJ: Technics Publications, 2010.

directed and controlled." IT governance recognizes information technology's role as an essential resource for creation, storage, use, and distribution of an organization's information assets and an indispensable source of competitive advantage for businesses and service delivery for government agencies and not-for-profit entities. The ISO/IEC 38500 standard treats IT governance as a component or subset of organizational governance. As such, IT governance is the responsibility of an organization's board of directors or other governing body. That view is shared by ISACA (originally known as the Information Systems Audit and Control Association), which formed the IT Governance Institute in 1998. Acknowledging this responsibility, some corporate boards have established a board-level IT committee on a level with audit, finance, and similar committees.

ISO/IEC TR 38502, *Information technology—Governance of IT—Framework and model*, differentiates IT governance from IT management, which is responsible for control and supervision of IT operations. IT governance is concerned with stewardship of information technology resources to ensure that they serve the interests of an organization's stakeholders. Control Objectives for Information and Related Technology (COBIT),[26] issued by ISACA, lists the key objectives of IT governance:

1. Strategic alignment to ensure linkage and compatibility of IT plans and organizational objectives.

2. Value delivery to ensure that IT supports the organization's legal and operational requirements and that anticipated benefits are realized.

3. Resource management to ensure optimization of the organization's technological infrastructure.

4. Risk management to recognize, assess, and mitigate risks associated with IT operations.

5. Performance measurement to monitor strategy implementation, project completion, process performance, and service delivery.

IT governance and information governance are allied concepts with complementary and compatible objectives. An organization's information technology function, as previously explained, is an important information governance stakeholder and an essential enabler for information-related strategies, initiatives, and activities. To fulfill its information governance responsibilities, the information technology function must itself be effectively governed. Information governance benefits if IT governance succeeds.

IT governance has a narrower focus than information governance. While information governance has a multidisciplinary scope, IT governance is limited to the initiatives and activities of a single stakeholder. Further, IT governance deals

---

[26] *COBIT 5: A Business Framework for the Governance and Management of Enterprise IT.* Rolling Meadows, IL: ISACA, 2012.

exclusively with digital information while information governance is concerned with information in all formats. In some respects, however, IT governance's scope is broader than its information governance counterpart. It deals with the acquisition and optimization of computer and networking hardware, software, labor, and purchased services that create, store, process, disseminate, and protect digital information. Information governance, by contrast, has limited involvement with technology resources, IT staffing, and purchased services. It is only interested in their impact on an organization's information assets.

Information Security Governance

As defined in ISO/IEC 27014, *Information technology—Security techniques—Governance of information security*, **information security governance** is the "system by which an organization's information security activities are directed and controlled." Like its information technology counterpart, the ISO/IEC 27014 standard considers an organization's board of directors or other governing body to have ultimate responsibility for information security governance. That view is shared by the IT Governance Institute, which treats information security governance as a specialized facet of IT governance; by the National Association of Corporate Directors (NACS), which recommends that information security be added to the governing board's agenda; and by the Corporate Governance Task Force of the National Cyber Security Partnership (NCSP), which issued a 2004 recommendation that advocated embedding information security in the corporate governance process.

The IT Governance Institute identifies the following basic outcomes of an information security governance initiative:

1. Strategic alignment with business strategy to support organizational objectives.

2. Appropriate measures to mitigate security risks and reduce potential impacts on information resources.

3. Efficient and effective utilization of an organization's information security knowledge and infrastructure.

4. Performance measurement to ensure that organizational objectives are achieved.

5. Optimization of information security investments.

These outcomes are similar to the COBIT objectives for IT governance presented in the preceding section, and they are fully compatible with information security's responsibilities as an information governance stakeholder. The close association of information security governance and IT governance recognizes the importance of digital information and threats posed by data breaches but that limited focus ignores security issues associated with physical records, which are significant information resources in many organizations. For alignment with information governance, the scope of information security governance must encompass information in all formats.

Risk Governance

As defined by the International Risk Governance Council (IRGC), a not-for-profit organization dedicated to understanding and managing risks, **risk governance** applies governance concepts to the identification, categorization, assessment, management, evaluation, and communication of risks. Risk governance is sometimes combined with corporate governance and compliance—an approach characterized as governance, risk management, and compliance (GRC). **GRC** is an umbrella discipline that combines governance, risk management, and compliance. OCEG, a nonprofit organization originally founded as the Open Compliance and Ethics Group, equates GRC with "**principled performance**," which it defines as the ability to "reliably achieve objectives (governance) while addressing uncertainty (risk management) and acting with integrity (compliance)."

This umbrella approach is designed to coordinate risk-related initiatives and promote sharing of information about enterprise risks across all three functions. Compliance violations expose an organization to fines and other penalties; stop-work orders, revocation of business or professional licenses, rejected applications for product approvals, or other disciplinary actions that can impede specific business activities; and, in extreme cases, criminal prosecution. Risk governance is widely recognized as a responsibility of an organization's governing board and executive management. Many corporate boards and other governing bodies have a risk committee that reviews an organization's risk strategies, policies, and processes.

The IRGC has developed a risk governance framework that includes the following components:

1. Pre-assessment to define and clarify a risk-related problem.

2. Appraisal based on a risk's measurable characteristics such as the probability of occurrence and the financial impact of adverse effects.

3. Evaluation to determine whether a risk is acceptable, tolerable with mitigation, or intolerable.

4. Management action to accept, reduce, transfer, or avoid a specific risk.

5. Communication to inform stakeholders affected by risk.

Because risk is an attribute of many organizational activities, risk governance affects and is affected by other governance initiatives. In particular, risk governance shares information governance's concerns about and involvement with information-related risk. The IRGC risk governance framework is compatible with risk management's responsibilities as an information governance stakeholder, but organizations are exposed to many risks that are not attributable to information-related policies, technologies, processes, or practices. Risk governance's mandate includes risks that are outside the scope of information governance. Examples include credit risks, liquidity risks, interest rate risks, exchange rate risks, and other financial risks; design risks, manufacturing risks, pricing risks, safety risks, patent infringement risks, and other risks associated with the development, sale, and use of products;

industrial health risks, workplace safety risks, employee benefit risks, and other employment-related risks; and risks associated with fire, destructive weather, vandalism, terrorism, environmental contaminants, and other hazards that may affect an organization's buildings or other property.

Process Governance

ISO 9000, *Quality management systems—Fundamentals and vocabulary*, defines a process as a "set of interrelated or interacting activities that use inputs to deliver an intended result," which may be a product or a service. ISO/TR 26122, *Information and documentation—Work process analysis for records*, defines a work process as "one or more sequences of transactions required to produce an outcome that complies with governing rules." According to ISO/IEC 33001, *Information technology—Process assessment—Concepts and terminology*, a process outcome is an "observable result of the successful achievement of the process purpose," which is defined as the "high-level objective of performing the process."

Process management encompasses the tasks required to develop processes and ensure that they accomplish their intended purposes. Process governance has the same relationship to process management that information governance has to information management. **Process governance** focuses, analyzes, and coordinates the process management initiatives and activities of an organization's functional units. A process governance framework includes the following components:

1. Guiding process management by reviewing policies, guidelines, procedures, and technologies associated with specific processes.

2. Establishing enterprise-wide standards for development and implementation of processes, including implementation methodologies, development platforms, and integration with other processes and resources.

3. Defining process-related roles and responsibilities.

4. Evaluating and prioritizing proposals for process-related initiatives to ensure alignment with organizational strategy and objectives.

5. Aligning process-related initiatives across functional units.

6. Developing performance measurements for process initiatives.

Process governance affects and is affected by the initiatives and activities of information governance stakeholders. Where business processes are involved, mutual alignment of process governance and information governance strategies and policies will have a beneficial impact on both disciplines. As defined in ISO 19439, *Enterprise integration—Framework for enterprise modelling*, a business process is a "set of enterprise activities that can be executed to achieve some desired end-result in pursuit of a given objective." Effective information governance is a precondition for successful implementation of business processes. At the same time, many information governance initiatives and activities involve business processes for creation, storage, retention, use, and distribution of information. **Business process management (BPM)** is a component of these information governance initiatives and activities. BPM is defined by the Association of Business Process Management Professionals as "a disciplined approach to identify, design, execute, document, measure, monitor, and control both automated and nonautomated business processes." By setting standards, priorities, and performance expectations for business processes, process governance supports and facilitates BPM activities.

While all business processes are information-dependent, process governance deals with agricultural processes such as planting, harvesting, fruit-picking, and irrigation; manufacturing processes such as casting, molding, forging, and machining; mining processes such as digging, drilling, blasting, and materials handling; and other processes where information plays a smaller role. Information governance has a limited impact on those processes.

Project Governance

According to ISO 21500, *Guidance on project management*, a project is a set of coordinated, controlled activities with starting and completion dates. This emphasis on the temporary nature of projects is in agreement with the definition presented in the Project Management Body of Knowledge (PMBOK) issued by the Project Management Institute.[27] Completion within an anticipated timeframe distinguishes business projects from business processes, which have no specified termination date.

The Association of Project Management (APM) defines **project governance** as a subset of corporate governance activities that are specifically related to project activities. APM distinguishes project governance from project management, which is concerned with the day-to-day execution of a project. The APM lists the following key components of project governance or, as APM characterizes it, governance of project management:

1. A governing board with overall responsibility for project management.

2. Clearly defined roles, responsibilities, and performance criteria for project management.

3. A project portfolio aligned with organizational objectives and capabilities.

4. Review and approval of proposed projects based on clearly defined outcomes and realistic business justification.

5. Stakeholders engaged in decision making at a level that reflects their roles in the organization.

6. Progress monitoring with closure of projects when they are no longer justified.

Information governance and project governance are intersecting disciplines. All projects are information-dependent. To accomplish its objectives, project

---

[27] *A Guide to the Project Management Body of Knowledge (PMBOK Guide)*. Newton Square, PA: Project Management Institute, 2013.

governance must have timely access to reliable information about the purpose, scope, progress, and outcomes of specific projects. Information governance contributes to these objectives. On the other hand, process governance has a beneficial impact on information governance. Many information governance initiatives involve nonrecurring projects with a defined scope and an anticipated completion date. Examples include development of records retention schedules, evaluation and selection of information management software, comparative analysis of in-house implementation vs. cloud-based services for specific computing functionality, threat and vulnerability assessment for specific information assets, and gap analysis for compliance with information-related laws and regulations. Data science responsibilities, as previously described, are principally project-oriented.

Innovation Governance

ISO 9000, *Quality management systems—Fundamentals and vocabulary*, defines innovation as a new or changed product, service, process, system, or other resource that realizes or redistributes value, generally with significant effects. Organizations must change and adapt to remain effective. For businesses, successful innovation is an important source of growth and competitive advantage. For government and not-for-profit entities, successful innovation yields improved service delivery and resource utilization. According to a 2012 study by the IESE Business School and Capgemini Consulting, the lack of a well-articulated innovation strategy and formal governance structure are among the most frequently cited constraints on an organization's ability to achieve its innovation targets.[28]

To address these concerns, **innovation governance** defines a framework and process to promote organizational effectiveness through innovation. An innovation governance program encompasses the following components:

1. Developing strategies, policies, standards, incentives, and rewards to promote innovation.

2. Establishing values and objectives that underpin innovation efforts.

3. Coordinating, prioritizing, and optimizing innovation-related investments across functional units.

4. Aligning innovation activities with organizational strategies and objectives.

5. Defining roles and responsibilities for innovation stakeholders.

Information governance can play an important role in innovation governance initiatives. To support creative thinking, timely access to reliable information is a requirement for research and development, the principal source of new and improved products and processes. For planning, decision making, and performance evaluation, innovation governance depends on current and historical information about an organization's business practices, customers, competitors, products, and services. Information technology, in particular, is a widely recognized source of innovation and a critical factor in innovation initiatives related to improved business processes. At the same time, innovation governance can help information governance formulate ideas for new and improved strategies, policies, and processes for creation, storage, use, distribution, and protection of an organization's information resources.

---

[28] Gapgemini Consulting and IESE Business School, University of Navarre, *Innovation Leadership Study—Managing Innovation: an Insider Perspective. https://www.capgemini.com/resources/ innovation-leadership-study—managing-innovation-an-insider-perspective/.*

6. Defining expectations and performance metrics for innovation activities.

7. Making decisions about resource allocation for innovation activities.

Some organizations have appointed a C-level executive—a chief innovation officer (CINO) or comparably titled official—to provide enterprise-wide leadership and accountability for innovation initiatives.

IG Maturity Analysis

A maturity model is an analytical tool for planning, assessing, and advancing a strategic initiative by measuring the maturity of an activity, operation, or business process. It is designed to describe and measure the status and progress of a program, process, or project over time.

A maturity model is a set of structured levels that define the characteristics associated with a particular activity. The characteristics represent varying degrees of formalization and effectiveness for the target activity. In particular, the characteristics reflect the integration of formalized policies and practices into an organization's operations.

As defined in ISO/IEC/IEEE 24765, *Systems and software engineering—Vocabulary*, a maturity model "describes an evolutionary improvement path from ad hoc, immature processes to disciplined, mature processes with improved quality and effectiveness." Most maturity models feature five or six levels that represent a hierarchy of formalization and effectiveness for a target activity. At the lowest level in the hierarchy, the target activity is guided by poorly defined, inconsistent practices, and formalization is limited or nonexistent. The highest level is characterized by optimized performance based on clearly articulated, well-tested policies and processes with a focus on continuous improvement. Intermediate levels in the maturity hierarchy represent progressively more effective stages between the two extremes. The third level typically represents a functioning target activity with an acceptable but not optimal degree of formalization. An organization's performance improves as it moves up the levels, but the highest level may not be desirable or attainable in every situation. For some organizations, the third or fourth level in a five-step maturity model represents an acceptable balance of formalization, effort, and cost.

A maturity model should be used at the inception of a target activity to determine the current state and establish a baseline for future measurement. The initial evaluation will identify gaps that must be addressed and actions that must be taken if the target activity is to move to the next maturity level. Subsequent evaluations will measure the activity's progress toward that goal.

Hundreds of maturity models have been developed for various purposes by academic researchers, professional associations, industry analysts, government agencies, and other organizations. Most of these models are patterned after the Capability Maturity Model (CMM), which was developed for the U.S. Department of Defense by Carnegie Mellon University's Software Engineering Institute (SEI) in the 1980s.[29] The CMM was intended for software development processes, but its basic principles and five-level maturity hierarchy have been adopted by models intended for other information-related activities. Maturity analysis is well suited to long-term initiatives like information governance, which can take several years to fully develop. The following sections describe maturity models that can be used to analyze information governance programs.

ARMA Maturity Model

The Information Governance Maturity Model developed by ARMA International is based on The Generally Accepted Recordkeeping Principles® (the Principles), which were issued by ARMA International in 2009, and updated in 2016, to foster general awareness of records management systems and standards and to assist organizations in developing effective programs for information assets and information governance. The Principles provide a set of eight recordkeeping principles, which are paraphrased next:

1. *Accountability*: A senior executive should be in charge of the information governance. The accountable executive will delegate program responsibility to appropriate individuals, adopt information governance policies and procedures to guide program personnel, and ensure that the program can be audited for compliance. A governance structure must be established for program development and implementation.

2. *Transparency*: An organization's recordkeeping processes and activities must be documented in an open and verifiable manner. Such documentation must confirm that the organization's recordkeeping policies and practices comply with applicable legal requirements and accurately and completely reflect the organization's activities. The documentation must be available to employees and appropriate interested parties.

3. *Integrity*: An organization's information assets must have a reasonable and suitable guarantee of authenticity and reliability. Recordkeeping processes, including audit processes, must provide reasonable assurance that the origin, time of creation or transmission, and content of recorded information are what they are claimed to be.

4. *Protection*: An organization's information governance program must protect information assets that are private, confidential, privileged, secret, or essential to business continuity. Recordkeeping procedures must provide appropriate protection controls from creation through final disposition of recorded information.

---

[29] The applicable standard is ISO/IEC 21827, *Information technology—Security techniques—Systems Security Engineering—Capability Maturity Model® (SSE-CMM®)*. Some researchers trace the maturity model concept to the five-level hierarchy of needs defined by the psychologist Abraham H. Maslow in an influential book entitled *Motivation and Personality* (New York: Harper Brothers, 1954). Maturity model developers adopted Maslow's view that satisfaction of lower level needs is a precondition for moving up the hierarchy.

5. *Compliance*: An organization's information governance program must comply with applicable laws, regulations, industry-specific rules of conduct, and other binding authorities related to creation, storage, retrieval, retention, disposition, dissemination, and protection of recorded information, as well as with the organization's own recordkeeping policies, procedures, and rules.

6. *Availability*: An organization's information assets must be organized, indexed, stored, and maintained in a manner that ensures timely, efficient, and accurate retrieval of information when needed.

7. *Retention*: An organization must retain information assets for an appropriate period of time to satisfy legal, regulatory, fiscal, operational, and historical requirements.

8. *Disposition*: An organization must provide secure and appropriate disposition for information assets that no longer need to be kept. In this context, disposition may involve destruction of information assets, transfer of information assets to another organization as part of a divestiture or other transaction, transfer of information assets to an archives or other scholarly repository, or transfer of information assets to clients or other parties who are the subjects of the information assets.

To characterize and evaluate information governance programs, ARMA's maturity model defines a five-level hierarchy based on these eight principles. As the Five-level Maturity Model in Figure 1 on the following page indicates, the maturity levels range from substandard to transformational:

- **Level 1.** Information governance and recordkeeping issues are addressed in a minimal, ad hoc manner, if they are addressed at all.

- **Level 2.** Recognition of the value of information governance and systematic recordkeeping is developing, but the organization's practices are poorly defined, incomplete, and marginally effective.

- **Level 3.** An organization's information governance and recordkeeping policies and practices are sufficient to satisfy legal, regulatory, and business requirements, but unaddressed opportunities for business process improvements and cost control exist.

- **Level 4.** Information governance issues and considerations are integrated into an organization's business decisions. Legal, regulatory, and business requirements are fully satisfied, and the organization is proactively pursuing information-related productivity improvements that promote efficiency and effectiveness.

- **Level 5.** Information governance is fully integrated into an organization's infrastructure, strategic initiatives, and business processes. Information governance is a recognized contributor to cost containment, client services, and competitive advantage.

The ARMA Maturity Model provides detailed descriptions for each recordkeeping principle at each maturity level. It is an excellent analytical tool for current

Figure 1

**5-Level
Maturity Model**

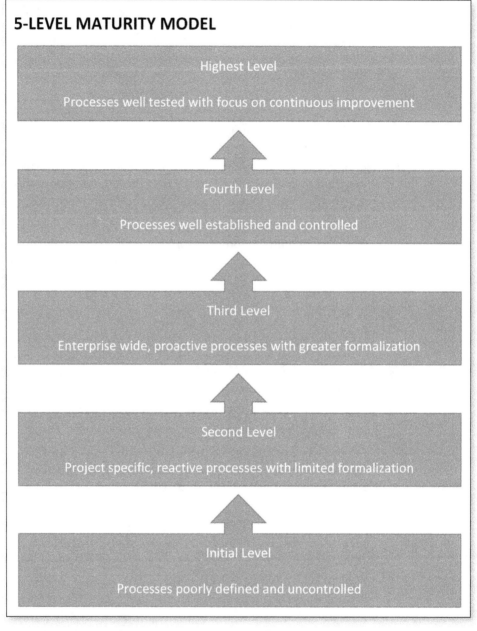

5-LEVEL MATURITY MODEL

Highest Level

Processes well tested with focus on continuous improvement

Fourth Level

Processes well established and controlled

Third Level

Enterprise wide, proactive processes with greater formalization

Second Level

Project specific, reactive processes with limited formalization

Initial Level

Processes poorly defined and uncontrolled

state assessment and gap analysis at the inception of an information governance initiative, and it can be re-applied at periodic intervals to measure an organization's progress.

Other Maturity Models

Although the ARMA Maturity Model is specifically designed to evaluate information governance initiatives in the context of systematic recordkeeping, useful maturity models have been developed by other organizations. These models address specific information governance components or related governance initiatives. Examples include the following:

1. ***The National Archives and Records Administration (NARA) in combination with the Federal Records Council has developed a maturity model to evaluate the effectiveness of U.S. government records management programs.***[30] The NARA model provides five maturity levels from absent to embedded formalization, with the mid-level representing a functioning program with some areas still under development. As a self-assessment tool for federal agencies, the NARA model evaluates maturity levels in three domains: (1) management support and organizational structure; (2) policy, standards, and governance; (3) and RIM program operations. In Australia, the Queensland State Archives has developed a maturity model that is based on the Queensland recordkeeping standard.[31]

- ***The COBIT process capability model developed by ISACA is based on the COBIT framework described in the previous section on IT governance.*** Designed to identify issues and set priorities for improved IT governance, the COBIT model defines six maturity levels ranging from nonexistent to optimized formalization.[32] At the mid-levels, an organization's IT governance processes are established, documented, and communicated but not monitored or measured for predictability. To move to the next step in the hierarchy, the requirements of the previous level must be completely achieved. The COBIT process capability model is compatible with ISO/IEC 15504-2, *Information technology—Process assessment—Part 5: An exemplar software life cycle process assessment model.*

- ***Various maturity models have been developed for data governance initiatives.*** Among the most widely cited examples, the Stanford Data Governance Maturity Model is a complex multidimensional hierarchy that defines qualitative and quantitative characteristics for specific aspects of data governance, including formalization of roles, responsibilities, policies and practices for data quality, data stewardship, metadata, and master data management.[33] The IBM Data Governance Council Maturity Model defines characteristics at five levels of maturity for 11 categories: organizational structure, data stewardship, policy, value creation, data risk management & compliance, information security & privacy, data architecture, data quality management, classification & metadata, information lifecycle management, and audit.[34]

[30] *Federal RIM Program Maturity Model User's Guide.* Washington: Joint Working Group of the Federal Records Council and National Archives and Records Administration, 2014. *https://www.archives.gov/records-mgmt/prmd/maturity-model-user-guide.pdf.*

[31] *Recordkeeping maturity model and road map: Improving recordkeeping in Queensland public authorities.* Runcorn, Queensland, Australia: Queensland State Archives, 2010. *http://www.archives.qld.gov.au/Recordkeeping/GRKDownloads/Documents/maturity_model_road_map.pdf.*

[32] *http://itgovernance.com/cobit5%20and%20iso15504.pdf* describes the COBIT levels.

[33] *http://web.stanford.edu/dept/pres-provost/cgi-bin/dg/wordpress/wp-content/uploads/2011/11/StanfordDataGovernanceMaturityModel.pdf.*

[34] *https://www-935.ibm.com/services/uk/cio/pdf/leverage_wp_data_gov_council_maturity_model.pdf.*

- *Several dozen maturity models for compliance and risk management have been developed by consulting firms, academic researchers, healthcare organizations, and others.* An online assessment tool developed by the Risk Management Society defines attributes and competency drivers for risk management programs at five levels of maturity.[35] The GRC Capability Model—developed by OCEG, a not-for-profit think tank that focuses on governance, risk, and compliance—defines characteristics that enable an organization to achieve its objectives while addressing uncertainty and integrity issues.[36]

- *An emerging group of maturity models addresses the data science function.* Examples have been developed by the Institute for Operations Research and the Management Sciences (INFORMS),[37] IBM,[38] the Data Science Association,[39] and The Data Warehousing Institute.[40]

- *A Digital Preservation Capability Maturity Model (DPCMM) is a five-level assessment tool that measures the maturity of an archival preservation program for electronic records.*[41] Maturity levels range from nominal, in which most electronic records that merit long-term preservation are at risk, to optimal, in which no electronic records are at risk. Intermediate levels are characterized by preservation of some but not all electronic records.

---

[35] *https://www.rims.org/resources/ERM/Pages/RiskMaturityModel.aspx.*

[36] *http://www.oceg.org/resources/red-book-3/.*

[37] *https://analyticsmaturity.informs.org/index.php.*

[38] *http://www.ibmbigdatahub.com/blog/maturity-model-big-data-and-analytics.*

[39] *http://www.datascienceassn.org/content/analytics-maturity-model.*

[40] *https://tdwi.org/pages/research/maturity-models-and-assessments.aspx.*

[41] Charles M. Dollar and Lori J. Ashley, *Assessing Digital Preservation Capability Using a Maturity Model Process.* April 2014. *http://static1.squarespace.com/static/52ebbb45e4b06f07f8bb62bd/t/53559340e4b058b6b2212d98/1398117184845/DPCMM+White+Paper_Revised+April+2014.pdf.*

Summary of Major Points

☑ Information governance defines strategies, policies, decision-making authority, accountability, and standards for an organization's information-related initiatives. As such, information governance is a focused aspect of organizational governance.

☑ Effective governance ensures that an organization will act diligently and prudently when making decisions about the acquisition, maintenance, use, and disposition of assets. Information governance enables organizational governance to fulfill its responsibility for stewardship of its highly valued information assets.

☑ An information governance framework defines the structure of an organization's information-related initiatives. All governance frameworks provide for a board, committee, or other governing body, but they differ in their definition of the role of governance and its relationship to management. The suitability of a given governance framework depends on a number of factors, including an organization's size, stakeholder interests, and corporate culture.

☑ Information governance develops high-level strategies, policies, and processes to support an organization's objectives. Stakeholders—business units or functional areas that deal with information—are responsible for implementing those strategies, policies, and processes in the context of specific information-related operations and delegated authority, subject to evaluation and oversight by information governance.

☑ An information governance framework identifies stakeholders and defines their roles and responsibilities. Depending on the organization, stakeholders may include, but are not necessarily limited to, records management, information technology, information security, risk management, compliance, legal affairs, data science, and archival administration.

☑ Information governance promotes interaction, cooperation, and consultation among stakeholders. It encourages dialogue, synergies, and consensus-building to balance the competing agendas of individual stakeholders, resolve conflicts, and achieve results that are in the common interest.

☑ Information governance must coexist and interact with other governance initiatives that deal with specific information-related matters or that have an impact on an organization's information-related policies and practices. Examples of such initiatives include data governance, IT governance, information security governance, risk governance, process governance, project governance, and innovation governance.

☑ Maturity models are analytical tools for planning, assessing, and advancing a strategic initiative. A maturity model can be used to assess the current state of an information governance initiative. It can identify gaps that must be addressed and actions that must be taken if an initiative is to move to the next maturity level. Maturity models have been developed for various purposes. The ARMA International Maturity Model is specifically designed for information governance assessments.

Part 2

Legal and Regulatory Requirements for Information Governance

All countries have laws and regulations that affect information governance initiatives. As a group, these laws and regulations support government oversight of an organization's information-related activities and operations. While their impact on corporations, partnerships, and other for-profit enterprises has been widely discussed, these laws and regulations apply to governmental and not-for-profit organizations as well. As explained in later sections, some laws and regulations apply exclusively to information that is created, collected, and maintained by government agencies.

Information is subject to laws and regulations in the governmental jurisdictions where it is created, collected, stored, or processed. This concept is sometimes characterized as **data sovereignty**. An organization's information-related policies and practices must comply with legal and regulatory requirements in all locations where it does business. The organization's headquarters location or the governmental jurisdiction in which it is incorporated or chartered is not the determining factor. A company, government agency, not-for-profit organization, or other entity is considered to operate in a given location if it has an office, employees, property, or—in the broadest interpretation—customers there.[42]

Among information governance stakeholders, records management, compliance, and legal affairs are typically responsible for identifying laws and regulations that impact an organization's information-related policies and practices in specific governmental jurisdictions. A large and growing number of legal reference sources are available online for this purpose. Many countries have government-operated databases of laws, regulations, ordinances, directives, and other legal instruments. These databases, which are publicly accessible through governmental websites,

---

[42] Some laws specify activities that do not constitute "doing business" in a given governmental jurisdiction. Examples from Section 191 of the California Corporations Code and Section 1301 of the New York Business Corporations Law include holding a meeting of a governing board, maintaining bank accounts, selling products through independent contractors, soliciting orders that require acceptance outside the state before becoming binding contracts, and maintaining, defending, or settling claims, disputes, or other legal proceedings.

contain the full texts of legal instruments, but a country's governmental system has a significant impact on information governance requirements and on the nature and amount of research that must be done to identify applicable laws and regulations:

- About 85 percent of the world's countries have a unitary system of government. A **unitary state** is a sovereign state governed as a single entity. In unitary states, national laws and regulations specify country-wide requirements. Subnational jurisdictions, where they exist, are limited to administrative responsibilities. They do not have legislative or regulatory authority that affects an organization's information-related policies and practices. Examples of unitary states include China, Japan, the United Kingdom, France, Italy, Spain, the Netherlands, Denmark, Norway, Sweden, Indonesia, and New Zealand.

- In a **federated country**, by contrast, a national government shares legislative and regulatory authority with subnational jurisdictions—states, provinces, territories, districts, counties, municipalities, and so on. Examples of federated countries include the United States, Canada, Mexico, Brazil, the Russian Federation, Australia, and India. Organizations that operate in federated countries are subject to national and subnational recordkeeping requirements. In the United States, for example, a given business operation or activity may be regulated at the national level, the state level, or both levels, and specific requirements can vary from location to location.

- Legal research to identify information-related laws and regulations is less complicated and requires less effort for unitary countries than for federated countries. In unitary countries, research is limited to national laws and regulations. For federated countries, thorough legal research must encompass national and subnational laws and regulations. In many countries, government websites provide searchable compilations of national laws and regulations, but online availability of subnational legislation varies from country to country. The United States, Canada, and Australia, for example, provide reasonably complete access to state and provincial laws and regulations.[43] Other federated countries offer limited online coverage of subnational jurisdictions.

- Some countries are member states of supranational political unions, which are formed to promote regional interaction and cooperation. Examples include

---

[43]   In the United States, recordkeeping requirements for business operations regulated by the federal government can be found in the U.S. Code, which is the codification by subject matter of the general and permanent laws of the United States, and, more commonly, in the Code of Federal Regulations (CFR), which is the codification of regulations issued by executive branch agencies of the U.S. government. The CFR is updated daily by the Federal Register. Recordkeeping requirements for business operations regulated by U.S. states and local governments can be found in compilations of statutes, codes, rules, and regulations issued by those jurisdictions. In Canada, Consolidated Acts and Consolidated Regulations cover federal requirements. Provinces and territories have their own laws and regulations. In Australia, the federal government provides online access to Commonwealth Acts and Regulations. Provinces and territories have similar compilations.

the European Union (EU), the Commonwealth of Independent States (CIS), the Organization for Harmonization of Business Law in Africa (OHADA), the Association of Southeast Asian Nations (ASEAN), the Caribbean Community (CARICOM), the Central American Integration System (SICA), and the Community of Portuguese-Speaking Countries (CPLP). For purposes of legal harmonization, some supranational entities have legislative authority over member countries that agree to transpose the supranational entity's legislation and directives into their own national laws. This harmonization can simplify legal research for organizations with business operations in multiple countries, assuming that member states adopt the supranational entity's legislation and directives without additions or other modifications.

- Some organizations must comply with information-related provisions in standards, guidelines, and codes of conduct issued by self-regulatory organizations (SROs), accrediting agencies, and other nongovernmental entities that exercise regulatory authority over specific industries or professions. Worldwide, thousands of such nongovernmental entities exist. Examples include the Financial Industry Regulatory Authority (FINRA), the Investment Industry Regulatory Organization of Canada (IIROC), the Mutual Fund Dealers Association (MFDA) of Canada, the United Kingdom Financial Conduct Authority (FCA), the International Federation of Pharmaceutical Manufacturers and Associations (IFPMA), the North American Electric Reliability Corporation (NERC), the Fair Labor Association (FLA), the American Medical Association (AMA), the American Bar Association (ABA), the Joint Commission, the College of American Pathologists, and the Middle States Commission on Higher Education.

Globally, tens of thousands of laws, regulations, standards, and guidelines contain provisions that may affect an organization's information-related policies and practices. Although a comprehensive survey is outside the scope of this book, the following discussion cites examples of pertinent laws and regulations in the following categories:

- **Recordkeeping requirements.** These requirements include laws and regulations that deal with collection, storage, retention, and disposal of recorded information.

- **Personally identifiable information data protection and privacy requirements.**

- **Information security requirements.** Security requirements include laws and regulations that mandate security planning, secure disposal of information, data breach notifications, and preparation of backup copies for specific information.

- **Information disclosure requirements.** Mandatory disclosure by government agencies, mandatory disclosure to government agencies, mandatory disclosure to data subjects, mandatory publication notification, court-ordered disclosure, and prohibited disclosure of nonpersonal information are included in information disclosure requirements.

- **Statutes of limitations.** These statutes affect information governance issues and activities.

The stakeholder impact matrix in Table 3 in Appendix C indicates which information governance stakeholders are directly affected by legal and regulatory requirements discussed in the previous categories. The impact of specific requirements on individual stakeholders is explained in the following sections.

Recordkeeping Requirements

All countries have laws, regulations, or other legal instruments that require organizations to create, collect, and retain records related to certain business activities and operations.

The principal purpose of these **recordkeeping requirements** is to ensure that information related to regulated activities and operations will be available for examination by auditors, investigators, inspectors, and other government officials. Failure to comply with recordkeeping requirements exposes an organization to civil or criminal penalties, including monetary fines, exclusion from participation in government programs, and—in rare cases—imprisonment.

The following sections survey recordkeeping requirements in the following categories:

1. Laws and regulations that require the creation or collection of information.

2. Laws and regulations that specify how long information must be kept.

3. Laws and regulations that mandate destruction of specific information.

4. Laws and regulations related to electronic recordkeeping.

5. Laws and regulations that specify the locations where information can and cannot be stored.

Information Creation/Collection Requirements

Some laws and regulations require an organization to create or collect certain information about its business activities, operations, and transactions. These laws and regulations have a direct impact on compliance and legal affairs, which are responsible for identifying, interpreting, and fulfilling the requirements, and on risk management, which must assess the impact that these requirements may have on an organization's risk profile. Records management, information technology, information security, data science, and archival administration are typically involved with information after it is created and collected.

Some laws and regulations in this category apply to a broad range of organizations. Others are sector specific. Examples include the following:

• **Registered corporation records.** Most countries have laws and regulations that specify the types of records that registered corporations must create. The Canada Business Corporations Act and the Canada Not-for-profit Corporations Act are typical. The records they require include articles of incorporation, bylaws, minutes of shareholder and committee meetings, shareholder and committee resolutions, annual financial statements, and registers of directors, officers, and shareholders. The Model Business Corporation Act, which has been adopted by the majority of American states, contains similar requirements, as do company laws in European and Asian countries.

- **Employee records.** Many countries have laws that mandate the creation or collection of certain employee information, including personal identification, dates of service, regular and overtime hours worked, wages, and paid and unpaid leave. In the United States, 29 CFR 516.2 specifies the information that every organization must keep about its employees. Similar information is mandated in Section 24 of the Canada Labour Standards Regulation, in Sections 3.32 through 3.40 of the Australian Fair Work Regulations, and in other national laws and regulations. These laws and regulations, which apply to all sectors, may be supplemented by laws that apply to employees in specific industries or business activities. In many countries, for example, hospitals are required to collect information about the education, experience, and other qualifications of their medical staff.

- **Securities trading records.** Many countries have laws and regulations that mandate the types of information to be created or collected by brokerage firms, investment advisers, and other companies or individuals involved in securities trading. In the United States, 17 CFR 240.17a-3 and SEC Final Rule on Books and Records Requirements for Brokers and Dealers under the Securities Exchange Act of 1934 (RIN 3235-AH04) specify the accounting records, transaction records, customer account records, complaint records, personnel records, and other information that must be created and maintained by national securities exchange members and by brokers and dealers who transact business in securities. Regulatory authorities in other countries have similar requirements.

- **Financial and/or banking records.** Most countries have laws requiring banks, credit unions, savings associations, and other financial institutions to maintain records that adequately identify their customers. In the United States, 32 CFR 1020.220 specifies the types of information that banks must collect about a customer at the time that an account is opened. Financial institutions must also indicate the documentation they used to verify a customer's identity. In Canada, guidelines issued by the Financial Transactions and Reports Analysis Centre (FINTRAC) specify customer identification information to be collected by financial institutions, life insurance companies, accountants, money services businesses, real estate companies, casinos, and dealers in precious metals and stones. Customer identification requirements for financial institutions in EU member states are covered in Directive 2005/60/EC on prevention of the use of the financial system for the purpose of money laundering and terrorist finance.

- **Medical records.** Some countries have laws that specify the personal and clinical information that hospitals, nursing homes, rehabilitation facilities, physicians, psychologists, and other healthcare providers must create or collect about their patients. In the United States, 42 CFR 482.24 specifies the types of personal and clinical information that hospitals must include in medical records as a condition of Medicare participation. Regulatory authorities in most American states impose similar requirements, as do Canadian and Australian provinces and territories.

Records Retention Requirements

All countries have laws and regulations that specify the period of time that certain business information must be kept. Among information governance stakeholders, these legally mandated records retention requirements have a direct impact on records management, which must consider recordkeeping laws and regulations when developing file plans, indexing schemes, and other mechanisms for organization and retrieval of recorded information, as well as lifecycle management policies and records retention schedules. Records retention laws and regulations also affect information technology, which is responsible for providing storage resources and implementing retention requirements for digital information in its custody or under its supervisory control; compliance, which must align an organization's records retention policies and practices with legal and regulatory requirements; risk management, which is concerned with the impact of noncompliance on an organization's risk profile; and legal affairs, which is responsible for providing legal interpretations, clarifications, and opinions about specific records retention requirements and practices.

Other information governance stakeholders are affected by an organization's records retention practices, but they are not involved in identifying, interpreting, or evaluating legal and regulatory requirements for recorded information. Archival administration must ensure the identification and preservation of records of scholarly value, but those determinations are based on research criteria rather than legal or regulatory requirements.

Records retention requirements apply to many types of information. Examples of retention requirements for widely encountered records include the following:

- **Business transactions and financial records.** Most countries have commercial codes, bookkeeping acts, and other laws that specify retention requirements for records that document an organization's business transactions and disclose its financial position. Examples include accounting books and ledgers, charts of accounts, balance sheets, financial reports, auditors' reports, records of goods purchased and sold, inventories, and supporting documentation such as contracts, invoices, payment vouchers, receipts, and reconciliation documents. Retention periods specified in laws and regulations range from 3 years to more than 10 years, depending on the country and the types of records involved. Retention periods for accounting records are also affected by statutes of limitations, which are discussed in a later section.

- **Tax records.** All countries have laws and regulations that specify retention requirements for information related to an organization's tax liabilities and payments. These requirements typically apply to all categories of direct and indirect tax levied by national and subnational jurisdictions, including income tax, payroll tax, sales tax, value-added tax, excise tax, and payroll tax. Generally, tax-related records must be kept as long as they are subject to audit by government regulators—depending on the country, 3 to 10 years following the end of the tax year to which the records pertain. In the United States, the standard period is three years after the original due date of the return or the date that the return is filed, whichever is later, but that time period is increased to six years where income is understated. Longer retention may be required for tax records relating to real estate purchases, capital improvements, certain deductions that are subject to recapture, and other matters.

- **Import/export records.** All countries have national laws and regulations that specify retention periods for import and export authorizations, customs certificates, transport documents, customs declarations, customs clearances, and other customs records. The required retention periods are typically short—five years or less in most countries.

- **Payroll records.** Most countries have laws and regulations that require employers to create and keep payroll information, including wages paid to and amounts withheld from individual employees. Depending on the country, typical retention periods range from three to six years.

- **Workplace health and safety records.** Some countries require employers to create and maintain information about workplace health and safety, including work-related accidents, occupational illnesses and injuries, employees' exposure to toxic chemical substances and biological agents, and inspection and testing of potentially hazardous equipment. In some countries, certain records must be retained for multiple decades. In EU member states, for example, records related to an employee's exposure to carcinogenic substances, mutagenic substances, or asbestos must be kept for 40 years after the exposure ceases.

- **Organizational records.** In many countries, laws and regulations specify retention requirements for a company's organizational records such as the minutes of a company's general and special meetings, lists of directors, registers of shareholders and bondholders, annual reports, and auditors' reports. Some countries also specify retention requirements for the records of liquidated companies, including closed branches of foreign companies.

The legal and regulatory requirements cited above apply to a subset of an organization's recorded information, but that subset can be voluminous; some organizations have large quantities of accounting, taxation, and employment records. A more extensive group of records retention requirements applies to specific industries or business activities that are closely monitored by regulatory authorities. In such situations, legally mandated retention requirements can affect a high percentage of organizational information. Banks, credit unions, and other financial services companies, for example, must retain information about their customers, individual transactions, and assets. Insurance companies must retain information about policies and claims. Hospitals, clinics, and other healthcare providers must retain information about patients. Pharmaceutical companies must retain extensive documentation about product manufacturing and testing. Airlines, railroads, and other transportation companies must retain information about equipment, facilities, authorized operators, and maintenance procedures. Sector-specific recordkeeping regulations are not limited to private entities. In the United States and many other countries, government agencies must comply with records retention requirements specified by archival authorities at federal and subnational levels.

Mandatory Destruction of Information

Recordkeeping laws and regulations typically specify minimum retention periods for the information to which they pertain. In most cases, the information can be kept longer than the minimum time period if warranted by operational needs or scholarly considerations, but some laws and regulations specify circumstances in which information must be destroyed after a period of time or when specified events occur. For example:

- In the United States, public school districts must destroy personally identifiable information about special education students at a parent's request when the information is no longer needed to provide educational services to the child.

- In some countries, criminal case information related to juvenile offenders must be destroyed after a specified period of time if certain conditions are met.

- Some countries mandate the destruction of information about unsubstantiated child abuse investigations, either immediately or after a specified period of time.

- Some countries have laws or regulations that mandate short retention periods and mandatory destruction for surveillance images produced by closed circuit television cameras or other video devices installed in public spaces.

- Data protection and privacy laws, which are discussed more fully next, typically mandate the destruction of information when it is no longer needed or, under certain conditions, when requested by the **data subject**; that is, the person to whom the information pertains. According to Article 17 of the European Commission's General Data Protection Regulation, which was adopted in May 2016 but becomes effective after May 2018, a data subject has a "right to be forgotten and to erasure" where personal data is no longer necessary for the purpose for which it was collected, where the data subject withdraws consent for processing, when the retention period consented to has expired, when the data subject objects to the processing of personal data for a given purpose. In such cases, an organization must erase the data without delay unless certain conditions apply. Exclusions are provided for reasons related to national security, national defense, public safety, prosecution of criminal offenses, scientific research, and avoidance of ethical breaches by regulated professions.

Mandatory destruction requirements affect all information governance stakeholders except archival administration, which deals exclusively with information that must be preserved permanently. Records management must consider mandatory destruction requirements when developing and implementing records retention schedules. Information technology must implement procedures to destroy digital information in its custody or under its supervisory control. As with records retention generally, compliance must align an organization's records destruction policies and practices with legal and regulatory requirements, while risk management is concerned with the impact of noncompliance on an organization's risk profile and legal affairs is responsible for providing interpretations, clarifications, and opinions about specific destruction laws and regulations. Data science may be required to destroy specific data associated with analytical projects.

- The constitutions of some Latin American countries contain "habeas data" provisions that allow data subjects to request destruction of incorrect information about them.

- Data protection laws in some non-EU countries specify maximum retention periods for records that contain personally identifiable information. In the Russian Federation, for example, Federal Law No. 152-FZ (On Personal Data) requires the destruction of personal data within 30 days after it is no longer needed for its original purpose. If that is not possible, access to the personal data must be blocked and the data destroyed within six months. According to the Serbian Personal Data Protection Act, personal data collected under a contract or on the basis of written consent must be deleted within 15 days of contract termination or withdrawal of consent. Personal data about a deceased person must be destroyed one year after the date of death.

Electronic Recordkeeping

Most recorded information originates in electronic format, and many paper records are scanned for storage and retrieval as digital images. Printing electronic records to produce paper copies for retention was a common practice in the twentieth century, but it is no longer a workable retention strategy. For economy and practicality, many organizations want to satisfy retention requirements with electronic records rather than paper documents.

Many laws and regulations permit the retention of records in electronic format as official copies.[44] Some electronic recordkeeping laws have been in effect for more than a decade:

- **15 US Code 7001(d)(3), Uniform Electronic Transaction Act (UETA), and the Code of Federal Regulations.** According to 15 US Code 7001(d)(3), electronic records can satisfy statutes and regulations that require the retention of a contract or other record "in its original form." Section 12 of the Uniform Electronic Transaction Act (UETA), which has been adopted by 47 states, the District of Columbia, Puerto Rico, and the U.S. Virgin Islands, contains virtually identical provisions.[45] Section 13 of the UETA provides that "evidence of a record or

---

[44] An official copy is the copy of a record that will satisfy an organization's retention requirements based on legal, operational, and historical considerations. Where the same record exists in multiple copies, one of the copies is designated the official copy to be retained for the indicated time period. Other copies are considered duplicate records for retention purposes.

[45] The nonadopting states (Illinois, New York, and Washington) have their own statutes pertaining to electronic transactions.

signature may not be excluded solely because it is in electronic form." Many sections of the Code of Federal Regulations and various state codes have been revised to accept electronic records to satisfy recordkeeping requirements.

- **Personal Information Protection and Electronic Documents Act (PIPEDA) and the Uniform Electronic Commerce Act in Canada.** PIPEDA[46] addresses the legal status of electronic documents as official copies to satisfy retention requirements. According to Article 37, electronic documents can satisfy records retention requirements specified in Canadian federal laws provided that the electronic documents are retained in their original formats or in a format that does not change the information they contain. Electronic documents must be readable by those entitled to access them, and they must be accompanied by information that identifies the origin and destination and the date and time that they were sent or received. Most Canadian provinces and territories have adopted the Uniform Electronic Commerce Act, which establishes functional equivalency rules that allow electronic records to satisfy legal requirements for written communications and recordkeeping.

- **The Commonwealth Electronic Transactions Act 1999 in Australia.** This act states that electronic records can satisfy retention requirements for written documents provided that they are readily accessible and useable for subsequent reference and the information they contain remains complete and unaltered except for the addition of an endorsement or immaterial changes that arise in the regular course of business. Australian states and territories have electronic transaction legislation that is compatible with the Commonwealth law.

- **Electronic transaction laws or electronic signature laws that affirm the legal status of electronic records in other countries.** These laws, which describe electronic records as electronic documents or data messages, draw upon model laws on electronic commerce and electronic signatures developed by the United Nations Commission on International Trade Law (UNCITRAL). They accept electronic records as official copies to satisfy retention requirements subject to certain conditions—the most common being that the electronic records must accurately preserve all content, the electronic records must remain readable throughout their retention periods, and printed copies must be provided when requested by government officials. Computer equipment and software to support retrieval, display, and printing must be available for as long as the electronic records are retained.

Electronic transaction laws apply to transactions associated with business and government operations. They do not address the legal status of electronic records that deal with noncommercial or nongovernmental matters, including such personal matters as powers of attorney, healthcare proxies, do-not-resuscitate orders (DNRs), and noncommercial trusts. In the United States, the Uniform Electronic

---

[46] As its title indicates, PIPEDA also deals with data protection. Those provisions are discussed in a later section.

Transactions Act specifically excludes wills or other testamentary instruments, records associated with certain transactions covered by the Uniform Commercial Code, and any records that are required by other laws or regulations to be in non-electronic format.

In some jurisdictions, electronic transactions and electronic signature laws exclude records related to adoptions, divorces, or family matters; pleadings, motions, and other official court documents; insurance cancellation notices; default notices associated with credit agreements; foreclosure and eviction notices; documents that require notarization; and records related to transportation or handling of hazardous substances. For most organizations, these exclusions will affect few, if any, electronic records. Additional exemptions may apply in specific situations. In New Zealand, for example, the Electronic Transactions Act 2000, approval of the chief archivist is required for retention of public records in electronic format. Some electronic transactions acts provide full or partial exemptions for existing laws that deal with specific matters.

Most information governance stakeholders are directly affected by electronic recordkeeping laws.

- Records management must consider them when developing retention guidance and advising business units about format requirements for official copies.

- Information technology must maintain the readability and usability of electronic records in its custody or under its supervisory control.

- Information security must implement procedures to ensure the integrity of electronic records throughout their retention periods.

- Risk management is concerned with the impact of noncompliance on an organization's risk profile.

- Compliance must align an organization's electronic recordkeeping practices with legal and regulatory requirements.

- Legal affairs must provide legal interpretations, clarifications, and opinions about specific electronic recordkeeping practices.

- Data science relies on electronic records for analytical projects, but it is not directly involved in the development of electronic recordkeeping policies.

- Archival administration is responsible for permanent preservation of electronic records of scholarly value.

Data Residency Requirements

Some laws and regulations restrict the geographic locations or governmental jurisdictions where specific information can be stored. These data residency requirements do not affect the storage of information in the country where information is created or collected, and they have no impact on organizations with business operations in a single country. They apply to multinational and transnational organizations that create or collect information in one country but want to store it in a different country.[47] Their principal purpose is to ensure that one copy of specific information is readily available to government officials for audits and investigations.

Some national laws require in-country retention of accounting and tax records. In many countries, certain employment and workplace safety and health records must be kept at a worker's place of employment. These data residency requirements do not necessarily prohibit out-of-country storage of backup copies or other duplicate records. As explained in the next section, data protection laws restrict or prohibit cross-border transfer of records containing personally identifiable information, where cross-border transfer is defined as sharing, transmitting, disclosing, providing access to, or otherwise making such information available to persons or organizations located in countries other than the country where the data was originally created or collected.

Data residency requirements limit or prohibit the centralization of information on network servers located at a regional center or headquarters site. In-country storage requirements have an impact on enterprise-wide implementations of content management systems, records management application software, email archiving systems, and other systems that support consolidated storage of electronic records. They also affect the use of cloud-based information services and the transfer of physical records to commercial storage providers located in other countries.

In multinational and transnational organizations, records management must consider data residency requirements when providing storage guidance and specifying storage arrangements for recorded information. Information technology is affected and possibly constrained by **data residency laws** or requirements that limit the locations where digital information can be stored. Compliance must align an organization's records storage practices with legal and regulatory requirements. Risk management is concerned with the impact of noncompliance on an organization's risk profile. Legal affairs must provide legal interpretations, clarifications, and opinions about specific storage practices. In multinational and transnational organizations, archival administration may need to decentralize its storage repositories for permanent records.

Data Protection and Privacy Requirements

Data protection laws, sometimes described as data privacy laws, *regulate the collection, use, and distribution of personally identifiable information (PII) by companies, government agencies, not-for-profit entities, and other organizations.*

---

[47] Multinational organizations are headquartered in one country but have branches or subsidiaries in other countries. Transnational organizations have distinct, autonomous operations in multiple countries. While multinational and transnational operations are closely associated with corporations and partnerships, many universities, scientific and medical research organizations, foundations, scholarly and professional associations, cultural institutions, philanthropic organizations, charities, religious groups, and other not-for-profit entities operate in more than one country.

- Data protection laws affect all information governance stakeholders. They directly impact the compliance function, which must align an organization's privacy policies and practices with legal and regulatory requirements; the information security function, which must develop and implement measures to protect personally identifiable information; the risk management function, which is concerned with the impact of data protection requirements on an organization's risk profile; and the legal affairs function, which is responsible for providing legal interpretations, clarifications, and opinions about data protection requirements and practices.

- Data protection laws also impact records management, to the extent that they affect retention periods and destruction practices for records that contain personally identifiable information, and the information technology function, which must implement safeguards to prevent unauthorized access to personally identifiable information in its custody or under its supervisory control. Data science must comply with data protection requirements for research projects that involve personally identifiable information.

- Data protection laws may restrict or prohibit access to some archival records that contain personally identifiable information.

As their name implies, data protection laws are designed to safeguard personally identifiable information and the interests of persons to whom the information pertains.

The following sections review the most important characteristics of data protection and privacy legislation. The discussion emphasizes laws that apply to personal information that is created, collected, stored, and used by various types of organizations. Some countries have additional laws and regulations for privacy and protection of personal information associated with specific businesses such as banks, brokerage firms, credit reporting agencies, and telecommunication service providers.

Definition of PII

ISO/IEC 29100, *Information technology—Security techniques—Privacy framework*, defines **personally identifiable information (PII)** as any information that can be used to identify a PII principal—a natural person to whom the personally identifiable information relates—or that might be directly or indirectly linked to a PII principal. European Union Directive 95/46/EC, the model for many data protection and privacy laws, defines personal data as any information that permits direct or indirect identification of an individual (the data subject). In particular, it mentions identification by reference to an identification number or to factors specific to an individual's physical, physiological, mental, economic, cultural or social identity. The European Union's General Data Protection Regulation, the replacement for Directive 95/46/EC, adds location data and online identifiers.

A widely cited report by the National Institute of Standards and Technology (NIST), a unit of the U.S. Department of Commerce, lists familiar data elements that can identify a person: name, Social Security number, date and place of birth, mother's maiden name, and biometric records along with educational, financial, and employment information that is linked or linkable to an individual.[48]

Various laws and regulations have expanded the range of PII to include additional types of information. For example, in the United States:

---

[48] E. McCallister et al., *Guide to Protecting the Confidentiality of Personally Identifiable Information (PII): Recommendations of the National Institute of Standards and Technology.* Special Publication 800-122. Gaithersburg, MD: National Institute of Standards and Technology, April 2010. *https://doi.org/10.6028/NIST.SP.800-122.*

- **45 CFR 164.514(b).** This federal regulation implements the Health Information Portability and Accountability Act (HIPAA), focuses on protected health information (PHI) as a type of PII. It lists the following data elements: name; street address, ZIP code, geocode, and other geographic subdivisions smaller than a state; telephone and fax number; email address; Social Security number; medical record number; health plan beneficiary number; account numbers; license number; license plate number and other vehicle identifiers; device identifiers and serial numbers; web URLs and IP addresses; fingerprints, voice prints and other biometric identifiers; full-face photographic or other images; and any other unique identifier.

- **16 CFR 312.2.** This federal regulation implements the Children's Online Privacy Protection Act (COPPA), includes screen names, instant messaging user identifiers, customer numbers held in a cookie, and files that contain a child's image or voice.

- **Title 1.8, Chapter 1, Section 1798.3 of the California Civil Code (the Information Practices Act of 1977).** This regulation defines personal information to include an individual's physical description, education, employment history, medical history, and statements made by or attributed to the individual. Section 1798.83(6)(A) of the California Civil Code, which deals with customer records, adds information about race, religion, political party affiliation, age and gender of children, and education as well as real property purchased, leased, or rented and the type of product or service purchased.

EU Requirements

Pending its anticipated replacement by the previously cited General Data Protection Regulation, Directive 95/46/EC is the basis for data protection requirements in member states of the European Union. Directive 95/46/EC and the General Data Protection Regulation differ in their implementation method and jurisdictional scope:

- *Directive 95/46/EC provides a consistent approach to data protection across the European Union by replacing national data protection laws and regulations that vary from country to country.* As with other EU directives, member states have implemented Directive 95/46/EC by transposing (incorporating) its provisions into their national laws. Unlike directives, EU regulations do not require transposition. When it is approved, the General Data Protection Regulation will be immediately applicable to EU member states, although certain aspects of data protection—such as employment law, professional secrecy laws, and personal data related to criminal offenses—will continue to be governed by national laws.

- *Directive 95/46/EC applies to companies, government agencies, not-for-profit entities, and other organizations that process personal data in an EU member state.* The General Data Protection Regulation has a broader scope: It applies to any organization that processes personal data in an EU member state; any organization that is subject to the national law of any member state by virtue of public international law, the set of legal rules governing international relations between sovereign entities; and any organization that offers goods or services to EU residents or that monitors the behavior of EU residents, regardless of whether the organization has a physical presence in the European Union.

Directive 95/46/EC defines processing of personal data to include collection, recording, organization, storage, alteration, retrieval, consultation, use, disclosure by transmission or dissemination, and erasure or other destruction. Personal data can be processed with the unambiguous consent of the data subject. Consent is not required if the processing is necessary for performance of a contract involving the data subject, for compliance with a legal obligation, to protect the vital interests of the data subject, or to perform a task carried out in the public interest. Data subjects have the right to obtain information about the purpose of an organization's processing of their personal data, the types of data being processed, and the recipients or categories of recipients to whom the personal data is disclosed. Data subjects have the right to prohibit processing of incomplete or inaccurate data, to object to processing of personal data for purposes of direct marketing, and to be informed when personal data is disclosed to third parties for purposes of direct marketing. The General Data Protection Regulation adds the data subject's right to information about the retention period for personal data and the right to erasure of personal data, as noted in a preceding section.

Directive 95/46/EC contains special requirements for processing sensitive personal data, which includes information about an individual's racial or ethnic origin, political opinions, religious or philosophical beliefs, trade-union membership, health, or sex life. The General Data Protection Regulation adds genetic data and data about criminal convictions, which some EU member states have included in national data protection laws. Directive 95/46/EC prohibits processing of sensitive personal data unless one of the following conditions apply: (1) the data subject has given explicit consent; (2) the processing is necessary to carry out obligations and rights related to employment law; (3) the processing is necessary to protect the vital interests of the data subject; (4) the processing is carried out in the course of legitimate activities by a foundation, association, or other not-for-profit entity; (5) the processing is performed by a healthcare professional for diagnosis, care, or treatment;(6) the processing is necessary to establish, exercise, or defend legal claims; or (7) the processing involves data that is publicly available. The General Data Protection Regulation also allows processing of sensitive personal data for historical, statistical, or scientific purposes, subject to appropriate protections.

As specified in Directive 95/64/EC, personal data must not be retained longer than necessary for the purposes for which it was collected or for which it is further processed. This well-established data protection principle first appeared in the Convention for the Protection of Individuals with Regard to Automatic Processing of Personal Data issued by the Council of Europe in 1981. Interpretation is required to determine the purpose for which personal data was collected in the context of specific business operations and the point when the data is no longer needed for that purpose. An organization needs personnel records that contain personal data about active employees, for example, but some of those records remain useful after termination of employment—to confirm prior employment when authorized to do so, to expedite the rehiring process for a former employee, to administer benefit programs for retired employees, and so on. Similarly, a university needs records that contain PII about enrolled students, but some of those records remain useful following graduation—to document a former student's courses and degrees for employment, for graduate school admission, or for other purposes. In these examples, some but not all personal data may require long retention to satisfy the purpose for which it was collected, but indefinite retention does not appear to be compatible with the data protection directive.

In some EU member states, national data protection laws have additional requirements that affect retention of personal data. In France, for example, personal data relating to a prospective customer cannot be retained longer than three years after the date of collection or the last contact with the prospect unless the prospect indicates a continued desire to receive commercial solicitations. The Germany Data Protection Act requires deletion of data relating to racial or ethnic origins, political opinions, religious or philosophical convictions, union membership, sexual matters, health, or criminal or administrative offenses for which the accuracy cannot be proven. In the Netherlands, the Exemption Decree to the Personal Data Protection Act specifies maximum retention periods for personal data created for certain business purposes such as access to buildings and computer systems, statistical or scientific research, sale of goods or services, and provision of legal or financial services to clients. In Finland, the continued need for personal data must be re-evaluated at five-year or shorter intervals.

Directive 95/64/EC prohibits cross-border transfer of personally identifiable information to countries that lack an adequate level of protection unless the data subject consents to the transfer, the transfer is mandated by a contract that is in the interest of the data subject, the transfer involves information that is publicly available, the transfer is mandated by legal proceedings, or the transfer is in the national interest. This prohibition applies to electronic records that may be transferred to servers operated by an organization's centralized information technology unit or by a cloud-based storage provider in another country. It also applies to paper records and other physical storage media, including backup or archival tapes that may be transferred to a commercial storage provider or an in-house records storage facility in another country.

Adequate protection is typically defined as the same level of data protection provided in the originating country. Where personal data originates in a member state of the European Union, it can be transferred to any other member state for retention. Personal data can also be transferred to Iceland, Liechtenstein, and Norway, which are members of the European Economic Area. The European Commission has identified other countries that offer an acceptable level of protection. Such countries include Andorra, Argentina, Canada, Switzerland, Faeroe Islands, Guernsey, Israel, Isle of Man, Jersey, New Zealand, and Uruguay. In late 2015, the European Union Court of Justice ruled that the United States-

European Union Safe Harbor Framework, an initiative of the U.S. Department of Commerce that defined privacy principles to which participating organizations must agree, was invalid for cross-border transfer of personal information between EU member countries and the United States. In 2016, the European Commission and the United States approved a new data transfer framework, the EU-US Privacy Shield, which provides stronger monitoring of U.S. companies by the U.S. Department of Commerce and the Federal Trade Commission. The new agreement also limits access to transferred information by law enforcement and national security agencies in the United States.

Directive 95/64/EC requires EU member states to impose penalties for violations of data protection principles, but the details are left to national laws. The General Data Protection Regulation specifies penalties ranging from 250,000 euros or 0.5 percent of annual net sales revenue for an organization's failure to implement an adequate mechanism for data subjects to exercise their rights to 100 million euros two to five percent of annual net sales revenue for processing personal data without a valid purpose and other serious violations.

Canadian Requirements

In Canada, the Privacy Act regulates collection, use, and disclosure of personal information by federal government agencies. For information maintained by provincial government agencies, similar laws combine privacy protection with freedom of information requirements, which are discussed in a later section.

The Personal Information Protection and Electronic Documents Act (PIPEDA)—previously discussed in relation to electronic recordkeeping—specifies requirements for collection, use, and disclosure of personally identifiable information by private sector organizations in Canada. PIPEDA applies to any nongovernmental organization that collects, discloses, or uses personally identifiable information in the course of commercial activities.[49] These organizations include associations, charities, religious groups, advocacy groups, and other not-for-profit organizations to the extent that they engage in commercial activities such as the sale of membership lists or donor lists. PIPEDA is a federal law. Some Canadian provinces have data protection laws that apply more broadly to not-for-profit organizations.[50]

PIPEDA defines personal information as information about an identifiable individual, but it specifically excludes the individual's name, title, business address, and business telephone number. Like other personal data protection laws, PIPEDA

---

[49] Collection, use, and disclosure of personal information by federal government agencies in Canada is regulated by the Privacy Act (R.S.C., 1985, c. P-21).

[50] Alberta, British Columbia, and Quebec have laws that apply to private sector organizations that do business in those provinces. The Office of the Privacy Commissioner of Canada considers these laws substantially similar to PIPEDA with respect to privacy protection. Ontario, New Brunswick, and Newfoundland and Labrador have privacy laws that are considered substantially similar to PIPEDA for protection of health-related information. Substantially similar data protection laws take precedence over PIPEDA for collection, use, or disclosure of personal information within a province or territory. PIPEDA is the regulatory authority for personal information that flows out of the province or territory to which a given law applies.

imposes significant restrictions on collection, use, and disclosure of personal information:

- **Purposes for collecting personal information.** PIPEDA requires organizations to identify and document the reasonable purposes for which personal data is collected. Personal data, including personal health information, must not be collected, used, or disclosed for other purposes.

- **Consent for collecting personal information.** PIPEDA requires the data subject's consent, but consent is not required if collection is clearly in the interests of the data subject and timely consent cannot be obtained; the collection is needed to investigate a breach of an agreement or a violation of the law; the information is contained in a witness statement that is necessary for an insurance claim; the collection involves information produced by the data subject in the course of employment and is consistent with the purpose for which the information was produced; the collection is solely for journalistic, artistic, or literary purposes; the information is publicly available; or the collection is made for purposes of making a disclosure required by law.

- **Consent for use of personal information.** PIPEDA prohibits the use of personal information without the data subject's knowledge or consent unless the information is needed for an investigation of a crime; the information is needed in an emergency to protect the life or health of the data subject; the information is contained in a witness statement that is necessary for an insurance claim; the information is produced by the data subject in the course of employment and is consistent with the purpose for which the information was produced; the information is used for statistical or scholarly purposes, provided that confidentiality is assured and the data subject's consent cannot be obtained; the information is publicly available; or the information was created more than 100 years ago or 20 years after the death of the data subject.

- **Personal information disclosures.** PIPEDA prohibits disclosure of personal information without the data subject's knowledge or consent unless the information is used to collect a debt, to comply with a court order, to respond to a request by a government institution that is authorized to obtain the information in relation to national security or legal matters, or to communicate with the data subject's next of kin, authorized representative, or other person in the event of an emergency; the information is produced by the data subject in the course of employment and is consistent with the purpose for which the information was produced; the information is contained in a witness statement that is necessary for an insurance claim; the information is used for statistical or scholarly purposes, provided that confidentiality is assured and the data subject's consent cannot be obtained; the information is publicly available; or the information was created more than 100 years ago or 20 years after the death of the data subject.

- **Personal information and employment relationships.** PIPEDA permits collection, use, or disclosure of personal information that is necessary to establish, manage, or terminate an employment relationship, provided that the data subject was informed that this collection, use, or disclosure will or may be done.

These requirements are compatible with principles specified in CAN/CSA-Q830-96, *Model Code for the Protection of Personal Information,* which was issued by the Canadian Standards Association in 1996 and is incorporated into PIPEDA as Schedule 1. CAN/CSA-Q830-96 specifies that personal information must be destroyed, deleted, or made anonymous when no longer needed for its identified purpose. In this respect, PIPEDA is comparable to EU data protection laws. CAN/CSA-Q380.96 advises but does not require organizations to develop and implement guidelines with minimum and maximum retention periods for records that contain personal information.

Of particular importance for archival administration, PIPEDA provides that records of historical value can be transferred to an archival institution for purposes of conservation 100 years after the records were created or 20 years after the death of the individual to whom personal information applies, whichever occurs first. PIPEDA does not prohibit transfer of personal information outside of Canada for storage or processing, but organizations are held accountable for protecting personal information associated with such transfer arrangements. The out-of-country entity is responsible for providing a comparable level of protection for personal information that it receives.

U.S. Requirements

The United States does not have a single data protection authority or an omnibus data protection law. Privacy and data protection are regulated by multiple agencies and addressed in multiple laws that apply to specific organizations or specific situations. Examples include the following: [51]

- **PII and federal government agencies.** The Privacy Act of 1974 (5 U.S.C. 552a), the most frequently cited example, applies to personally identifiable information that is collected, used, or distributed by federal government agencies. The Privacy Act does not apply to other organizations. Federal government agencies must limit their recordkeeping to personally identifiable information that is relevant and necessary. Agencies must establish appropriate safeguards to ensure the confidentiality and security of personally identifiable information, and they must make reasonable efforts to notify data subjects when information is disclosed in connection with a compulsory legal process. Data subjects have the right to request amendment of their personally identifiable information to address inaccurate, irrelevant, or incomplete content.

- **PII and state and local government agencies.** Privacy laws with similar restrictions apply to personally identifiable information maintained by state and local

---

[51] For a more complete survey, see Virginia A. Jones, *Requirements for Personal Information Protection, Part 1: U.S. Federal Law,* Pittsburgh: ARMA International Educational Foundation, October 2008, *www.armaedfoundation.org/pdfs/FederalPrivacy.pdf,* and Virginia A. Jones, *Requirements for Personal Information Protection, Part 2: U.S. State Laws,* November 2009, *www.armaedfoundation. org/pdfs/Requirements_for_Personal_Information_US_States.pdf.*

government agencies. According to Section 1798.14 of the California Civil Code, for example, state government agencies must only collect and maintain personal information that is relevant and necessary to accomplish an agency's purpose. Section 94 of the New York State Personal Privacy Protection Law (Public Officers Law, Article 6-A) contains similar provisions. Executive Order 00-03 requires Washington state government agencies to protect the confidentiality of sensitive personal information. Among its provisions, it limits the collection of personal information to data that is reasonably necessary for government operations, and it instructs agencies to examine their retention schedules and retain personally identifiable information only as long as needed for the purpose for which it was originally collected or the minimum period required by law.

- **PII and business and other organizations.** Some states have laws that address the security of personally identifiable information maintained by businesses and other organizations. Most of these laws deal with personal information in the context of consumer protection. As discussed in a later section, these information security laws mandate disposal of personally identifiable information in a manner that renders the information unreadable or undecipherable by any means.

- **Specific categories of PII.** The federal government and some states have laws that deal with collection and disclosure of specific categories of personally identifiable information such as protected medical information,[52] customer information maintained by financial institutions,[53] customer data,[54] student records,[55] records that identify library users,[56] records related to video rentals,[57]

---

[52] The HIPAA Privacy Rule (45 CFR Part 164) limits the use and disclosure of protected health information. It applies to patient records and other personal health information maintained by health plans, health care clearinghouses, and health care providers that conduct health care transactions electronically.

[53] As specified in 15 U.S. Code 6801, financial institutions have an "affirmative and continuing obligation" to protect the security and confidentiality of customers' nonpublic personal information. The Financial Services Modernization Act of 1999, commonly known as the Gramm-Leach-Bliley Act (GLBA), requires financial institutions to give customers a privacy notice indicating the types of personal information it collects and the types of businesses to which that information may be disclosed. Customers can refuse to have their personal information shared under certain circumstances.

[54] The Fair and Accurate Credit Transaction Act (FACTA) gives data subjects the option of stopping a company's affiliates from sharing customer information for marketing purposes.

[55] The Family Educational Rights and Privacy Act (FERPA) requires written permission from students or parents of minor students to release information from educational records subject to exclusions specified in 34 CFR 99.31.

[56] The American Library Association lists privacy laws related to library records. *www.ala.org/advocacy/privacyconfidentiality/privacy/stateprivacy*.

[57] The Video Privacy Protection Act (18 U.S. Code 2710) was passed after the *Washington City Paper* published the video rental records of Judge Robert Bork, a Supreme Court nominee. The newspaper obtained the information from a video rental store. A 2011 amendment, which was supported by Netflix and other entertainment companies, allows disclosure if the data subject provides a blanket

court records,[58] information about licensed drivers of motor vehicles,[59] information about children collected by website operators and online services,[60] and personal information held by Internet service providers[61] and telecommunication service providers.[62]

Data Protection in Other Countries

The data protection laws of European countries that are not members of the European Union generally follow the EU model. These countries include Iceland, Liechtenstein, and Norway, which are part of the European Economic Area but are not EU member states, and in countries, such as Montenegro and Bosnia and Herzegovina, that are seeking membership in the European Union. Several dozen countries in Asia, the Middle East, Africa, and Latin America have laws that limit collection, use, and distribution of personally identifiable information. Most of these data protection laws follow the EU model. As previously noted, the European Union recognizes certain countries as providing a level of data protection that satisfies requirements specified in Directive 95/46/EC.

Like Canada, Australia has a combination of federal and state legislation that regulates the collection, use, and distribution of personally identifiable information. At the federal level, the Australian Privacy Act 1988 presents privacy principles that apply to Australian and Norfolk Island government agencies, certain private sector companies and not-for-profit organizations, and all private healthcare providers. The Australian Privacy Act does not apply to government agencies in Australian states and territories, which have their own data protection legislation.

In New Zealand, the Privacy Act 1993 applies to all governmental and nongovernmental entities. New Zealand also has codes of practice that specify privacy requirements for specific industries, such as credit reporting and telecommunications, or types of information, such as healthcare information.

---

written consent. The original law required the data subject's consent at the time the disclosure was sought.

[58] The National Center for State Courts has compiled a list of laws relating to privacy and public access to court records.
http://www.ncsc.org/topics/access-and-fairness/privacy-public-access-to-court-records/state-links.aspx.

[59] The Driver's Privacy Protection Act prohibits the disclosure of personal information contained in motor vehicle records maintained by state governments without the consent of the data subject, subject to exceptions specified in 18 U.S. Code 2721.

[60] The Children's Online Privacy Protection Rule (16 CFR 312) requires parental consent prior to disclosure of personal information about children under 13 years of age.

[61] The National Conference of State Legislatures provides links to privacy laws related to Internet service providers. *http://www.ncsl.org/research/telecommunications-and-information-technology/state-laws-related-to-internet-privacy.aspx.*

[62] Under the Electronics Communications Privacy Act (ECPA), telecommunication service providers must not intentionally divulge the contents of any communications they transmit unless the originator or address consent to the disclosure, or certain other conditions apply. The Stored Communications Act specifies penalties, including fines and imprisonment, for violations.

Information Security Requirements

Various laws and regulations specify security requirements for certain information maintained by companies, government agencies, not-for-profit entities, and other organizations.

Among information governance stakeholders, these laws and regulations have a direct impact on: (1) the information security function, which has principal responsibility for developing plans and measures to ensure the security, confidentiality, and integrity of an organization's information assets; (2) on information technology, which is responsible for implementing security measures for digital information in its custody or under its supervisory control; (3) on records management, which must incorporate security considerations into policies and procedures for retention, destruction, storage, and retrieval of physical records; (4) on the compliance function, which is responsible for aligning an organization's information security initiatives with legal and regulatory requirements for disposal of sensitive information; (5) on risk management, which is concerned with the impact of data breaches and other information security events on an organization's risk profile; and (6) on the legal affairs function, which is responsible for providing legal interpretations, clarifications, and opinions about an organization's information security requirements and practices. While data science and archival administration are not involved in the development of information security policies and procedures, they must comply with them for information related to their responsibilities.

Security Planning Requirements

Some countries have laws and regulations that require organizations to develop and implement security plans to protect information in their custody or under their supervisory control, including information maintained by cloud-based services or other third-party providers. Some of these laws and regulations are sector-specific:

- **FTC Safeguards Rule (16 CFR 314) and HIPAA Privacy Rule (45 CFR 164.530).** Widely cited U.S. examples include the FTC Safeguards Rule (16 CFR 314), which applies to customer information maintained by financial institutions over which the Federal Trade Commission has jurisdiction, and the HIPAA Privacy Rule (45 CFR 164.530), which applies to health plans, health care clearinghouses, and health care providers that electronically transmit health information.

- **The Federal Information Security Modernization Act of 2014 (FISMA).** This act requires U.S. government agencies to develop, implement and assess security plans for information and information systems that support agency operations and assets.

- **The Payment Card Industry Data Security Standard (PCI DSS).** This standard is a global industry regulation issued by the PCI Security Standards Council,

Information security laws and regulations do not mandate specific methods or technologies. They typically state that an organization must implement reasonable and appropriate measures to protect information against unauthorized disclosure, use, alteration, and destruction. Such measures may involve technological approaches, such as user account access controls, cryptography, and intrusion detection software; administrative procedures, such as well-defined acceptable-use policies, compliance monitoring, and employee training; and physical security precautions, such as locking server rooms and records storage areas when unattended, timely destruction of decommissioned storage devices and obsolete media, and regular maintenance and testing of fire suppression mechanisms.

specifies security requirements for merchants, financial institutions, and other organizations that accept or process bankcards for payment transactions.

- **European Union Directive 95/64/EC and national privacy and data protection laws.** Security requirements specified in European Union Directive 95/64/EC and in comparable national privacy and data protection laws apply to all organizations but focuses on requirements and safeguards to prevent unauthorized use or disclosure of personal information.

Data Disposal Requirements

Data disposal requirements affect all information governance stakeholders except archival administration, which deals exclusively with permanent information:

- *The data protection laws discussed previously mandate secure destruction of personally identifiable information when it is no longer needed for the purpose for which it was originally collected.* This is the case with Directive 95/64/EC and its counterparts in EU member states and other countries. The African Union Convention on Cyber Security and Personal Data Protection conforms to the EU model in mandating destruction of personal information when no longer needed for the purpose for which it was collected or further processed. According to the Australian Privacy Act 1988, federal government agencies and nongovernmental organizations must take reasonable steps to destroy personal information or render it anonymous when it is no longer needed. According to the New Zealand Privacy Act, an organization cannot retain personal information longer than necessary for the purpose for which it was collected. The Japanese Act on the Protection of Personal Information does not mandate destruction of personal information when no longer needed, but a data subject can request deletion of personal information that was acquired or processed in violation of the law.

- *Some U.S. laws and regulations require destruction methods that render information unreadable and unusable.* As an example, the FTC Disposal Rule (16 CFR 682.3), which is part of the Fair Credit Reporting Act, applies to any organization or individual that uses credit scores, employment histories, insurance claims, medical histories, and other consumer reports to determine eligibility for credit, employment, insurance, or other purposes. It also applies to service providers that process or maintain consumer information. The FTC Disposal Rule does not specify destruction methods, but it does list acceptable examples, including shredding and burning for paper records and erasure or physical destruction for electronic media.[63] According to guidance issued by the U.S. Department of Health and Human Services, HIPAA-compliant destruction methods for protected health information include shredding of hard copy media and clearing, purging, or other sanitization of electronic media in a manner consistent with guidelines issued by the National Institute of Standards and Technology (NIST).[64]

• *A number of states have passed data disposal laws for consumer information and other personally identifiable information maintained by companies, not-for-profit entities, and other organizations that are not covered by sector-specific requirements.*[65] Some of these laws mandate specific disposal methods. The New Jersey Statute on Methods of Destruction of Certain Customer Records (N.J. Stat. § 56:8-162, 2013) is typical in requiring destruction of customer records by "shredding, erasing, or otherwise modifying the personal information in those records to make it unreadable, undecipherable, or non-reconstructable through generally available means."

• *According to the Personal Information Protection and Electronic Documents Act, organizations that do business in Canada must exercise care when disposing of personal information to prevent unauthorized access, but no method of destruction is specified.* A guidance document on disposal principles and best practices issued by the Office of the Privacy Commissioner of Canada lists acceptable methods, including physical destruction of paper records or electronic media, overwriting of information, and degaussing of magnetic media.

Data Breach Notification Requirements

ISO/IEC 27040, *Information technology—Security techniques—Storage security*, defines a **data breach** as a compromise of security that leads to accidental or unlawful access to or destruction, loss, alteration, or unauthorized disclosure of protected data that is transmitted, stored, or otherwise processed. Data breaches may involve lost or stolen paper documents, removable storage devices and media, or mobile computing devices; unauthorized access to databases or other electronic records; unintended disclosure of information to unauthorized persons; or other incidents that involve potential misuse of personally identifiable information, including protected health information and payment card information.

---

[63] Failure to comply exposes an organization to FTC enforcement actions. In 2007, a mortgage company paid a $50,000 penalty for failure to dispose of consumer information properly. In 2009, a pharmacy chain agreed to settle FTC charges that it had improperly disposed of financial and medical information about its customers. In 2012, two payday lending and check cashing companies paid $101,500 for improper disposal of consumer documents.

[64] R. Kissel et al., *Guidelines for Media Sanitization.* NIST Special Publication 800-88, Revision 1. Gaithersburg, MD: National Institution of Standards and Technology, December 2014. *http://nvlpubs.nist.gov/nistpubs/SpecialPublications/NIST.SP.800-88r1.pdf.*

[65] The National Conference of State Legislatures has compiled a state-by-state list of data disposal legislation with links to individual laws. See *http://www.ncsl.org/research/telecommunications-and-information-technology/data-disposal-laws.aspx.*

Data protection laws typically require organizations to safeguard personally identifiable information and prevent data breaches. An increasing number of laws and regulations mandate notification of data breaches to the affected data subjects and regulatory authorities:

- **Data breach notification requirements in the United States.** In the United States, the majority of states and territories have data breach notification laws.[66] At the federal level, sector-specific laws and regulations include data breach notification requirements. As an example, the HIPAA Breach Notification Rule (45 CFR Part 164, Subpart D) requires covered entities and their business associates to notify the affected individuals and the Secretary of Health and Human Services about any impermissible use or disclosure that compromises the security or privacy of protected health information. Where more than 500 residents of a state or jurisdiction are involved, prominent media outlets must also be notified.[67] The FTC Health Breach Notification Rule (16 CFR 318) specifies requirements for non-HIPAA-covered entities that maintain electronic personal health records.

- **Financial institution required notifications.** According to the Interagency Guidelines Establishing Information Security Standards issued by the Federal Deposit Insurance Corporation (FDIC Rules and Regulations, Appendix B to Part 364), financial institutions must notify customers of security incidents that involve unauthorized access to or use of personally identifiable information, including any combination of components that allow someone to access a customer's account. Federally insured credit unions have similar requirements for member notification, as specified in 12 CFR 748, Appendix A.

- **Data breach requirements in Canada.** The Digital Privacy Act amended the Personal Information Protection and Electronic Documents Act to require prompt and conspicuous notification of data breaches involving personally identifiable information where there is "a real risk of significant harm to the individual." Some Canadian provinces have laws that require data breach notification.

- **Personal data breach requirements in Europe.** As specified in European Commission Regulation No. 611/2013 on the measures applicable to the notification of personal data breaches under Directive 2002/58/EC of the European Parliament and of the Council on privacy and electronic communications, providers of public electronic communication services, including telecommunication service providers and Internet service providers, must notify national

---

[66] The National Conference of State Legislatures has compiled a state-by-state list of security breach legislation with links to individual laws. See *http://www.ncsl.org/research/telecommunications-and-information-technology/security-breach-notification-laws.aspx*.

[67] As required by the Health Information Technology for Economic and Clinical Health (HITECH) Act, the Department of Health and Human Services has posted a list of over 1,400 HIPAA data breaches that have affected more than 500 individuals since 2009. The listed incidents involved unauthorized disclosure, theft, or other incidents involving physical and electronic records. See *https://ocrportal.hhs.gov/ocr/breach/breach_report.jsf*.

authorities and adversely affected individuals about all personal data breaches. In some EU member states, national data protection laws require organizations to notify data subjects if misuse of personal data may cause significant damage. Some EU member states and other European countries have national data breach notification laws for specific sectors such as financial services and healthcare. In 2016, the Netherlands introduced a general notification requirement that applies to all breaches involving personal data.

- **Data breach notification requirements in Asia.** Several Asian countries, including Japan, have data breach notification requirements that apply to specific sectors such as financial services. Under the South Korean Personal Information Protection Act, regulators must be notified about data breaches that involve more than 10,000 individuals. In Taiwan, the Personal Information Protection Act specifies that affected individuals must be notified about unauthorized disclosure, theft, or other data breaches.

Among information governance stakeholders, data breach notification requirements have an obvious impact on the information security function, which has front-line responsibility for security incidents; on compliance, which must align notification procedures with legal and regulatory requirements; on risk management, which must assess the risks associated with data breaches; on legal affairs, which must deal with the legal implications of data breaches and provide interpretations, clarifications, and opinions about notification requirements when data breaches occur.

Information Backup Requirements

ISO 22300, *Societal security—Terminology*, defines business continuity as the ability to continue delivering products or services at acceptable predefined levels following a disruptive incident. As discussed in ISO/IEC 27040, *Information technology—Security techniques—Storage security*, backup copies support business continuity by ensuring the recoverability of essential information assets following an adverse event. As an information security requirement, many countries have laws, regulations, and guidelines that mandate the creation and storage of backup copies of information for business continuity purposes. For the most part, these information backup requirements are sector-specific. Examples include the following:

1. In the United States, HIPAA administrative safeguards specified in 45 CFR 164.308 require covered entities and business associates to create and maintain "retrievable exact copies of electronic protected health information."

2. As specified in Appendix G of the business continuity planning component of the FFIEC Information Technology Examination Handbook issued by the Federal Financial Institutions Examination Council (FFIEC),[68] financial

---

[68] *Business Continuity Planning Booklet.* IT Examination Handbook. Federal Financial Institutions Examination Council, February 2015.
    http://ithandbook.ffiec.gov/ITBooklets/FFIEC_ITBooklet_BusinessContinuityPlanning.pdf.

institutions must maintain onsite and offsite backup copies to provide disaster recovery capabilities.

3. According to FINRA Rule 4370 (Business Continuity Plans and Emergency Contact Information) issued by the Financial Industry Regulatory Authority, all firms and brokers that sell securities to the public must have written business continuity plans that include provisions for backup of electronic and hardcopy information.

4. According to CFTC Rule 23.603 issued by the Commodity Futures Trading Commission (17 CFR 23.603), commodity swap dealers and major swap participants must backup essential data and documents and store the backup copies offsite in either paper or electronic formats.

5. In an industry guidance document for clinical trials, the Food and Drug Administration states that electronic records must be backed up regularly, and that the backup copies should be stored in a secure location, typically "offsite or in a building separate from the original records."[69]

6. NERC Standard CIP-009-1, *Cyber Security—Recovery Plans for Critical Cyber Assets*, issued by the North American Electric Reliability Corporation, a federally recognized authority that develops and enforces reliability standards for electrical grids, requires industry-wide implementation of processes and procedures for backup and storage of mission-critical information maintained by users, owners, and operators of bulk power systems. Backup media must be tested annually or more often to ensure the continued availability of information.

7. As specified in GST/HST Memorandum 15.1, General Requirements for Books and Records (June 2005), Canada Revenue Agency requires creation of backup copies by all entities subject to the Excise Tax Act.

8. According to Section OM-5.7.2 of Volume 1 of the Central Bank of Bahrain Rule Book, copies of a bank's vital records must be stored offsite and be "readily accessible for emergency retrieval."

9. According to Article 16 of Bank of Israel Regulation No. 357, Proper Conduct of Banking Business: Information Technology Management, banking corporations must take measures to "ensure the possibility of reconstructing information from backup copies." Backup copies must be kept at a location that is "distant from the original storage location."

10. According to Article 23 of the Risk Management Regulation, Version 2.0 (December 2008) issued by the Saudi Arabian Monetary Agency's Insurance Supervision Department, an insurer must store backup copies of all data.

11. According to Article 307.1 and 307.4 of Ultima Circular No. 2077 issued by the Central Bank of Uruguay in February 2011, financial institutions must create at least two weekly full backup copies of accounting data sufficient to reconstruct their operations and financial statements.

---

[69] *Guidance for Industry: Computerized Systems Used in Clinical Investigations* (May 2007). *http://www.fda.gov/OHRMS/DOCKETS/98fr/04d-0440-gdl0002.pdf.*

12. In Argentina, Disposition 11/2006, Security Measures for the Treatment and Maintenance of the Personal Data Contained in Files, Records, Databanks, and Databases, requires backup copies for sensitive personal data. Such copies must be stored in a secure repository at a reasonable distance from the original data.

These backup laws and regulations have a direct impact on information technology, which must produce and store the backup copies of digital information at prescribed intervals. In many organizations, records management is responsible for backup arrangements for physical records. Compliance must ensure that an organization's backup practices are aligned with legal and regulatory requirements. Risk management must assess the role of backup copies in mitigating risk. Legal affairs must provide interpretations, clarifications, and opinions about information backup requirements and practices. In some organizations, information security develops backup policies that information technology and records management must implement. Data science and archival administration are not directly affected by information backup requirements.

Information Disclosure Requirements

Many countries have laws and regulations that mandate the disclosure of certain information by companies, government agencies, and not-for-profit organizations in specific circumstances.

These information disclosure requirements include:

1. **Freedom of information laws**, which give the public a legal right to access information maintained by government agencies.

2. Laws and regulations that require organizations and professions to disclose information to government agencies when certain events occur.

3. Laws and regulations that give individuals access to information maintained about them by government agencies, educational institutions, healthcare providers, and other organizations.

4. Laws and regulations that require organizations to disclose information to the public.

5. Laws and procedural rules that mandate disclosure of information in response to court orders.

These information disclosure requirements affect all information governance stakeholders. Compliance and legal affairs are usually directly involved in evaluation and approval of disclosure requests. Risk management must assess the impact of disclosure requirements and requests on an organization's risk profile. Records management, information technology, data science, and archival administration may be involved in the identification, retrieval, analysis, delivery, or other processing of requested information. Information security is concerned with disclosure-related activities that have implications for the security or integrity of information.

Disclosure by Government Agencies

About half of the world's countries have laws or constitutional provisions that give the public access to information held by government agencies:

- In the United States, the Freedom of Information Act (FOIA) gives the public the right to request information held by federal government agencies. Certain information related to criminal law enforcement, national security, and foreign intelligence is excluded. The FOIA process is not centralized. Individual federal agencies respond to FOIA requests that they receive. Response time depends on the nature and amount of information requested and the agency's backlog of pending requests. Agencies can charge a fee for lengthy searches and extensive reproduction of information. To facilitate public access to information, federal agencies make frequently requested data and documents available on their websites.

- All American states and the District of Columbia have enacted similar laws that require disclosure of public records held by state and local government agencies.[70] Subject to variations from state to state, these laws typically provide exclusions for proprietary business information, unwarranted invasions of personal privacy, law enforcement records, and attorney-client communications.

- In Canada, the Access to Information Act provides public access to information held by federal government institutions. Exclusions include information that was given to federal institutions in confidence by another government, information that might be injurious to governmental or internal affairs, information that might endanger national defense or security, and certain law enforcement information. Canadian provinces have enacted similar laws that apply to information held by provincial and local government agencies, subject to exclusions that vary from jurisdiction to jurisdiction.

- The Council of Europe Convention on Access to Official Documents recognizes a general right of access to information held by national, regional, and local governments, subject to exclusions for national security, defense, and personal privacy. A subset of Council of Europe member states have signed the convention, but some EU member states have enacted their own freedom of information laws.

- The Australian Freedom of Information Act 1982 provides access to information held by federal government ministers and agencies. All Australian states and territories have comparable laws.

---

[70] The National Freedom of Information Coalition provides links to state laws. See *http://www.nfoic.org/state-freedom-of-information-laws*.

- New Zealand has two right-to-know laws: the Official Information Act 1982, which applies to information held by the national government, and the Local Government Official Information and Meetings Act 1987.

- In India, the Right to Information Act 2005 provides access to information held by the central government, as well as state and local governments. Other Asian examples include the Japanese Law Concerning Access to Information Held by Administrative Organs, enacted in 1999; the Taiwanese Freedom of Government Information Law, enacted in 2005; and the South Korean Act on Disclosure of Information by Public Agencies, enacted in 1996.

Disclosure to Government Agencies

Freedom of information laws require disclosure of public records by government agencies. Laws discussed in this section require disclosure of information to law enforcement, regulatory authorities, or other government agencies when certain events occur. Depending on the circumstances, disclosure may involve submission of a form or written report accompanied by data or documents related to the event.

These event-based disclosure requirements are in addition to periodic filings, reports, or other submissions required by sector-specific regulatory authorities.[71] They also differ from laws and regulations that require certain organizations and professions to disclose information about their products or services to specific groups such as consumers, home buyers, borrowers, students, clients, or patients. Event-based disclosure requirements are sector-specific. In some cases, event-based disclosures relate to potentially criminal matters. Examples of these mandatory disclosure requirements include the following:

- Most countries have antimoney laundering or antiterrorism laws that require banks and other financial institutions to report suspicious financial transactions.

- Many countries have laws and regulations that require publicly traded companies to disclose information about their financial condition or events in specific circumstances—for example, to correct or update previously disclosed information that is no longer accurate or complete.

- Many countries require pharmaceutical companies to report information about adverse events that occur during clinical trials of unapproved drugs, biological products, and medical devices to regulatory authorities.

- Some countries have laws that require manufacturers, importers, distributors, and retailers of consumer products to report defects that pose substantial risk of injury or that fail to comply with applicable product safety rules.

- Most countries require healthcare providers and clinical laboratories to report information related to certain infectious diseases to protect public health and welfare.

---

[71] Companies that issue securities for sale to the public, for example, must make regular reports to national regulatory authorities about their financial condition, operating results, management compensation, and other matters.

- Many countries have laws that require healthcare providers, educators, social workers, caregivers, and others to report suspected maltreatment of children, the disabled, the elderly, or other vulnerable persons.

- Some countries have laws that require healthcare providers to report information about domestic violence injuries or sexual assaults.

- Some countries have laws and regulations that require an organization to provide written notification about critical or fatal workplace injuries and occupational illnesses.

- Some countries have laws and regulations that require an organization to provide written notification the appropriate government agency about chemical spills, oil spills, or other accidents or incidents that threaten the public health or the environment.

- In the United States, 48 CFR 52.203-13, Contractor Code of Business Ethics and Conduct, requires federal government contractors to make written disclosures related to credible evidence of violations of the civil False Claims Act or federal criminal laws involving fraud, conflict of interest, bribery, or gratuity. This disclosure requirement remains in effect for three years after final payment on a contract.

Disclosure to Data Subjects

Freedom of information laws have a significant impact on information governance policies and practices, but their authority is limited to government agencies. They do not apply to information that is created, collected, or maintained by nongovernmental organizations.

By contrast, most of the data protection laws discussed in a preceding section allow data subjects to obtain personal information that is created, collected, or maintained about them by governmental and nongovernmental organizations, including companies and other for-profit entities. European Union Directive 95/46/EC, which is the model for many data protection laws, affirms a data subject's right to access personal information in order to verify its accuracy and confirm that it is being correctly used for the purpose for which it was originally collected. Data subjects can request correction of errors in their personal information. This "right to rectification" also allows a data subject to make a supplemental statement where personal information is incomplete.

In the United States and elsewhere, sector-specific laws and regulations give data subjects the right to access specific information maintained about them. Among the many examples that might be cited:

- As specified in 45 CFR 164.524, the Health Information Portability and Accountability Act gives data subjects the right to access medical information maintained about them by healthcare providers and other HIPAA-covered entities, subject to exclusions for psychotherapy notes and information compiled in reasonable anticipation of civil or criminal proceedings. U.S. state laws contain similar provisions as do the personal health information laws of some Canadian

provinces. In countries with omnibus data protection laws, medical information maintained by healthcare providers is treated like other types of personal
information. It is available to the data subject unless an exclusion applies. Some
data protection laws provide an exclusion where a healthcare entity reasonably
believes that giving access would endanger the health of the data subject or
where the record contains information that was given to the healthcare entity
with an obligation of confidentiality.

- In the United States, the Family Educational Rights and Privacy Act gives
students and the parents of minor students the right to inspect and review education records maintained about them by schools, higher educational institutions, and state educational agencies. Exclusions include educational records
that contain information about more than one student, financial records, and
confidential letters and statements of recommendation where the student has
waived the right to inspect those letters and statements. Students and parents
also have the right to request correction or removal of inaccurate or misleading
information contained in education records. Other countries have similar laws.
In Canada, for example, Section 266(4)(b) of the Ontario Education Act gives
students and their parents the right to access their educational records and to
request the correction or removal of inaccurate information.

- According to the Fair Credit Reporting Act, a consumer reporting agency
that collects, evaluates, or disseminates information about a consumer's credit
worthiness must give data subjects access to all information maintained about
them at the time of the request, including the sources of the information, the
identity of persons who procured a consumer report for employment or other
purposes during the preceding 24 months, and inquiries received by the agency
in the past 12 months. Canadian provinces and territories have similar laws.[72] In
Australia, Section 19 the Privacy (Credit Reporting) Code gives data subjects the
right to access information held by credit reporting agencies and credit providers.

- According to the Children's Online Privacy Protection Act, which was cited
previously, operators of websites and online services must give parents access to
personal information collected about their children under 13 years of age.

Mandatory Public Notification

Some laws and regulations specify that organizations must notify the public
about certain events or activities. These public notification requirements can be
satisfied through publication of the information in newspapers, distribution of the
information through broadcast media outlets, making the information available
on websites, posting the information in publicly accessible locations, making the
notification at a public meeting, or in other ways. Public notification laws and
regulations typically apply to a narrow range of information:

---

[72] The Canadian Office of Consumer Affairs provides links to information sources at
http://www.consumerinformation.ca/eic/site/032.nsf/eng/01112.html.

- Many countries have laws that require registered companies to disclose certain information to the public. EU Directive 2009/101/EC is typical in mandating public disclosure of a company's incorporation documents, officers, registered office location, annual accounting documents that must be published in accordance with EU directives, and liquidation proceedings. In some countries, professional associations, charities, and other not-for-profit organizations are required to disclose specific information to their members, but in organizations with large memberships disclosing information to their members is equivalent to public disclosure.

- In some countries, banks must notify the public when specific events occur. In the United States, for example, the Federal Deposit Insurance Corporation requires banks to make a public disclosure when it plans to establish or relocate an office.

- Some countries have "right to know" laws that mandate disclosure of information about hazardous chemicals to which the public may be exposed. In the United States, for example, the Emergency Planning and Community Right to Know Act (42 U.S. Code 11004) requires chemical manufacturing facilities to immediately notify the public about the accidental release of certain toxic substances.

- In the United States, the Safe Drinking Water Act requires water utilities to notify customers when a problem with their drinking water occurs. The notification must include information about the contaminants involved, the date the sample was collected, the potential adverse health effects, and the population at risk.

- In some countries, property owners, real estate developers, and others who are planning commercial or residential construction projects must publicly disclose information about the purpose, scope, and characteristics of proposed projects.

- In the United States, 42 U.S. Code 16918 and various state laws mandate public disclosure via a government-operated website of selected information about registered sex offenders. This requirement differs from disclosure in response to an inquiry under a freedom of information law. In Canada, certain provinces notify the public about the release of convicted sex offenders from prison.

Court-ordered Disclosure

Many countries have laws that require an organization to disclose information requested by government officials for use in a civil or criminal investigation. While some government agencies can use administrative subpoenas or similar instruments to obtain information without judicial oversight,[73] most disclosures are made in response to a court order that specifies the information to be provided. In

---

[73] Various U.S. laws authorize the use of administrative subpoenas to compel disclosure of information in criminal and national security investigations. Examples include the Controlled Substances Act, the Inspector General Act, the Stored Communications Act, the National Security Act, and the Fair Credit Reporting Act. For additional examples, see *http://www.justice.gov/archive/olp/ rpt_to_congress.htm.*

the United States, for example, the USA PATRIOT Act allows the Federal Bureau of Investigation to apply for a court order for "books, records, papers, documents, and other items" related to investigations of international terrorism. Similarly, the Antitrust Civil Process Act authorizes the U.S. Department of Justice to serve a "civil investigative demand" upon a company where an antitrust violation is suspected. In Canada, the Criminal Code allows law enforcement officials and other government authorities to use a production order to compel an organization to make financial records, telecommunications data, or certain other information available within a specified period of time.

Although disclosure for government investigations is a significant concern for information governance stakeholders, most court-ordered disclosure of information occurs in the context of discovery for civil litigation. Discovery is the investigative phase of civil litigation when the opposing parties can obtain information to help them prepare for trial. Discovery requirements are specified in civil procedure rules, which apply to specific jurisdictions. In the United States, Rule 26(b) of the Federal Rules of Civil Procedure covers discovery of nonprivileged matter that is relevant to a party's claim or defense. Most states have similar discovery provisions. In Canada and Australia, discovery is covered by federal court rules and by provincial, state, and territorial rules. In England and Wales, the rules of standard disclosure apply to most cases. Other countries have similar provisions for court-ordered disclosure of information for civil litigation.

Discovery often involves document production, which is broadly defined as a request for recorded information in paper or electronic formats. The term "documents" in this context encompasses computer data, video recordings, audio recordings, and other records that are not typically considered documents. The term "**e-discovery**" refers to discovery requests that involve these and other types of electronically stored information (ESI). Upon receipt of a discovery order, an organization must determine whether it has the requested information in its possession or under its control; retrieve the information from office areas, computer systems, warehouses, or other repositories where it is stored; review it for relevance; exclude information that is subject to attorney-client privilege, patient-physician privilege, state-secret or national security privilege, or other attributes that exempt it from discovery in specific situations; eliminate duplicate copies and irrelevant information; catalog the information to be disclosed; and record the information in an agreed-upon format on appropriate media for delivery to the requesting party. All of this must be done in a legally defensible manner, often on a tight schedule.

Of particular importance for legal affairs, compliance, and risk management, all parties involved in legal proceedings must comply fully and in a timely manner with court-ordered discovery. Failure to do so can have serious consequences, particularly if the requested information was destroyed without a satisfactory explanation. This type of records destruction can lead to charges of intentional or negligent destruction of evidence. Depending on the nature of the information and the party's perceived intent, the possible corrective actions include monetary

To minimize the risk of noncompliance, an organization must act promptly and decisively to preserve evidence by imposing a mandatory litigation hold on information deemed relevant for lawsuits, government investigations, arbitrations, or other legal proceedings. A litigation hold is a temporary suspension of destruction for information that may be relevant for litigation or government investigations. The hold must be implemented as soon as the organization receives a summons or complaint, when the organization is first on notice regarding possible legal proceedings, or when a prelitigation dispute or repeated inquiries about a specific matter suggests that legal proceedings can be reasonably anticipated. The organization's routine retention and disposal policies and practices will be temporarily suspended for information that is subject to a litigation hold. Such records will not be destroyed until the legal matters to which they relate are fully resolved and the litigation hold is rescinded, even if the records' retention periods elapse in the interim.

sanctions; adverse inference instructions in which a jury is allowed to infer that the destroyed records were harmful to the party that destroyed them, a default judgment in favor of the opposing party, and, at the extreme, criminal penalties for obstruction of justice.

Among information governance stakeholders, legal affairs is principally responsible for imposing and rescinding legal holds, but other information governance stakeholders are also involved. Drawing on its enterprise-wide familiarity with an organization's recordkeeping practices, records management often assists legal affairs in identifying business units and functional areas that are likely to have relevant information in their custody or under their supervisory control. Information technology must implement mechanisms to implement litigation holds for electronic records stored on in-house computers. It also works with cloud-based service providers to ensure the preservation of relevant information maintained off-premises. Archival administration could maintain historical information that is relevant for litigation, but, because such information is retained permanently for its scholarly or other research value, litigation holds are not required to ensure its preservation.

As an additional consideration, an organization may be subject to nonparty (third-party) discovery orders for legal proceedings when it is neither the claimant nor the defendant. Such nonparty discovery orders are routinely received by financial institutions, medical service providers, insurance companies, educational institutions, and companies with which a claimant or defendant has done business. Nonparty discovery requests obligate an organization to identify and produce relevant information for legal matters in which they have no direct interest. An organization may also receive a nonparty request to preserve information related to a particular matter that is the subject of actual or anticipated litigation. As a complicating factor, nonparties are not necessarily informed about resolution of the litigation covered by a discovery order or preservation request. Consequently, determining when its disclosure obligations end can be difficult.

Prohibited Disclosure of Nonpersonal Information

As previously discussed, data protection and privacy laws generally prohibit the disclosure of personally identifiable information, including protected health information, without the consent of the data subject. Many countries have laws and regulations that prohibit the disclosure of other types of information in specific circumstances. For example:

- The U.S. Criminal Code contains various prohibitions against disclosure of information. 18 U.S. Code 798 prohibits disclosure of classified information in any manner that imperils national security. According to 18 U.S. Code 842, disclosing any information pertaining to the manufacture or use of explosive, destructive devices in connection with a violent crime is a federal crime. As specified in U.S. Code 2511, intentionally disclosing the contents of an intercepted oral or electronic communication is illegal. Subject to some exceptions, 18 U.S. Code 2702 prohibits voluntary disclosure of customer communications by providers of electronic communication services. 18 U.S. Code 1905 contains a general prohibition against disclosure of confidential information by federal government employees and contractors.

- In the United States, trade secrets are protected by state laws. Many states have adopted versions of the Uniform Trade Secrets Act, which prohibits unauthorized disclosure or use of trade secrets, which are defined as information that derives actual or potential economic value from not being generally known and is subject to reasonable efforts to maintain its secrecy. The Canadian Uniform Trade Secrets Act contains similar provisions. In some countries, intellectual property statutes or common law prohibit disclosure of trade secrets.

- Organizations often use nondisclosure agreements, which are legally enforceable contracts, to restrict the dissemination of strategic plans, competitive intelligence, financial information, and other confidential business information.

- Many countries have insider trading laws that prohibit the unauthorized disclosure of nonpublic information about the plans or condition of a publicly traded company where such disclosure could confer a financial advantage related to the purchase or sale of the company's stock. In the United States, the Securities and Exchange Act of 1934 (15 U.S. Code 78u-1) prohibits insider trading. Examples of similar laws from other countries include the Canada Business Corporations Act, European Union Regulation No. 596/2014 on Market Abuse, the Swiss Stock Exchange Act, the Norwegian Securities Trading Act, the Japanese Financial Markets Abuse Act, and the Australian Corporations Act.

- Laws and rules of conduct prohibit certain professions from disclosing information that they acquire in the course of their work. Most countries have laws or precedents that recognize some form of attorney-client privilege for legal advice. Subject to some exceptions, attorneys cannot disclose any confidential communications related to representation of a current or former client without the client's informed consent. In limited circumstances, accountants, tax practitioners, and actuaries may be prohibited from voluntarily disclosing a client's financial or tax-related information without the client's permission, subject to certain exceptions. The Uniform Arbitration Act, which has been enacted by many states, allows an arbitrator to issue a protective order prohibiting the disclosure of specific information.

- In the United States, the Federal Reserve Board, Federal Deposit Insurance Corporation, Office of the Comptroller of the Currency, and other financial regulators prohibit banks and credit unions from disclosing reports of regulatory examinations, ratings, and other nonpublic supervisory information, without the permission of regulatory authorities. A similar prohibition applies to banks in Canada and some other countries.

Statutes of Limitations

Statutes of limitations—also known as limitations of action or periods of prescription—define the period of time during which a person or organization can sue or be sued.

Civil codes define statutes of limitations for breach of contract, personal injury, property damage, anticompetitive business practices, professional malpractice, libel, and other matters.[74] Penal codes define statutes of limitations for prosecution of felonies, misdemeanors, or other criminal violations. Limitations of assessment periods are the fiscal counterparts of statutes of limitations. They prescribe the period of time that a government agency can determine taxes owed. Once the period defined by a given statute of limitations or limitation of assessment has elapsed, no legal action can be initiated for a specific matter.

Among information governance **stakeholders**—business units or functional areas involved with or affected by an organization's information-related strategies, policies, or processes—statutes of limitations have a significant impact on risk management, legal affairs, and records management:

- **Risk management.** For risk management, statutes of limitations establish the risk window—the period of time that an organization is exposed to risks related to litigation, government investigations, regulatory compliance, tax audits, and other matters that expose an organization to costly legal proceedings, tax reassessments, penalties for compliance violations, or other adverse outcomes.

- **Legal affairs.** For legal affairs, statutes of limitations define the time period during which information needs to be available to address legal issues, answer queries, and resolve conflicts related to contracts, product liability, regulatory audits, labor relations, intellectual property, and other matters. Statutes of limitations also establish the time period during which information is subject to time-consuming, costly discovery requirements for legal proceedings.

- **Records management.** For records management, statutes of limitations define the period of time that records being retained in support of an actual or possible legal action can be used for that purpose. While they can have a significant impact on a given organization's records retention practices, the time periods specified by statutes of limitations are not equivalent to retention periods, but they do have an impact on retention decisions. Records need not be retained for the entire time periods specified by statutes of limitations, but doing so is often

---

[74] Some countries have a general statute of limitations for cases where a law does not specify a different time period. Such periods can be long—20 years or more—but the most common civil matters are typically covered by specific provisions.

prudent. If records are being retained specifically and solely to support legal actions, and they otherwise have no operational or historical value, retention periods longer than pertinent statutes of limitations serve no purpose.

Statutes of limitations begin when a specific event, such as a breach of contract or a personal injury, occurs. The limitation period depends on the type of legal matter involved and the circumstances of the case. For a given type of legal proceeding, statutes of limitations vary from country to country and, in some federated nations, from state to state. The following sections survey statutes of limitations for civil litigation related to commonly encountered business matters. Statutes of limitations for criminal offenses, such as fraud or breach of fiduciary duty, are outside the scope of this discussion.

Breach of Contract

A breach of contract occurs when one of the parties fails to fulfill the terms and conditions of a contract or other binding legal agreement. The contract may be oral or in writing, which is the typical scenario for companies, government agencies, not-for-profit organizations, and other legal entities. Written contracts are required for certain types of transactions such as the sale of real property, the sale of goods that exceed an amount specified by law, or the assumption of debt obligations of another party.

The party initiating a civil action for breach of contract must have information that confirms the existence, terms, and conditions of the contract. Depending on the circumstances, the wronged party can sue to compel fulfillment of the contract or to collect damages resulting from nonfulfillment. In the United States, the statute of limitations for civil litigation related to a breach of a written contract ranges from 3 to 15 years, depending on the state in which the litigation is initiated. Some states have a shorter limitation period for oral contracts. In some Canadian provinces, the statute of limitation period is as short as two years for certain contracts. In other countries, limitation periods for contract-related litigation generally range from 2 to 15 years, depending on the type of contract. Some countries have longer statutes of limitations for contracts related to the sale of real property or the construction of buildings and shorter statutes of limitations for contracts related to certain types of services such as transport of goods or repair of equipment.

Depending on the country, the statute of limitations for legal proceedings may begin when a breach occurs or when the breach is discovered. Typically, there is little difference between these triggering events because most breaches of contract become known soon after they occur. Where the triggering event is discovery of the breach, some countries impose an absolute statute of limitations as a maximum time period to initiate legal proceedings—10 years from the signing of a contract, for example—which avoids an indefinite risk window for litigation.

Personal Injury

Personal injuries—including bodily injuries and emotional distress, possibly leading to death—can be caused by vehicular accidents, workplace accidents and illnesses, property hazards, assaults by persons or animals, defective products, malfunctioning equipment, exposure to unsafe environmental conditions, medical errors, or other harmful events or situations. Where a personal injury is attributable to negligence, the injured party may sue for medical expenses, lost wages, pain and suffering, or other damages. Personal injury lawsuits, which account for the majority of civil litigation in the United States, are a significant source of risk for companies, government agencies, and not-for-profit organizations. They can result in high legal expenses, time-consuming legal discovery, and very large jury awards. Complex cases can involve multiple plaintiffs, multiple defendants, and multiple jurisdictions.

Statutes of limitations for personal injury of an adult plaintiff range from one year to six years in most jurisdictions, although it can be several decades in some countries. In most American states and Canadian provinces, the limitation period is three years or less. For injuries involving children, the limitation period begins when the injured party attains age 18. Regardless of age, the limitation period typically begins when the injured party becomes aware, or should reasonably have become aware, of the injury. This increases the risk window in product liability cases. Information about products being developed, tested, manufactured, or sold today may be relevant for legal actions several decades in the future. In some countries, statutes of repose specify a maximum time period, usually 10 years, based on the date on which a given product was initially introduced, regardless of when the plaintiff became aware of the injury.

Property Damage

Property damage can involve damage to a building, vehicle, equipment, or other property owned by an individual or organization. Property damage may be caused by fire, flooding, accidents, neglect, human error, criminal behavior, natural disasters, or other adverse events. The defendant may be a negligent party or an insurance company that refuses to pay a claim. Statutes of limitations for litigation related to property damage range from 1 year to 10 years from the date on which the damage occurred. In most American states and Canadian provinces, the statute of limitations is six years or less. Some countries have a longer statute of limitations for litigation relating to damage to buildings or land.

Employment Discrimination

Litigation related to employment discrimination can pose significant risks for companies, government agencies, and not-for-profit organizations. Such litigation may involve multiple plaintiffs and can result in large monetary awards and high legal costs.

In the United States, statutes of limitations provide a relatively small risk window for employment disputes related to discrimination claims. For federal violations based on Title VII of the Civil Rights Act of 1964, the Americans with Disabilities Act (ADA), the Pregnancy Discrimination Act (PDA), or the Genetic Information Nondiscrimination Act (GINA), an employee must first file a complaint with the Equal Employment Opportunity Commission (EEOC), which must complete its investigation within 180 days in most cases. If the EEOC disallows the claim, it will issue a Notice of the Right to Sue. This notice allows the claimant to pursue civil litigation, which must commence within 90 days of receiving the EEOC Notice.

A Notice of the Right to Sue is not required for civil litigation based on violations of the Age Discrimination in Employment Act (ADEA). Such litigation can be initiated 60 days after an EEOC complaint is filed but not later than three years from the date that the alleged discrimination occurred for claims based on willful violations (where the employer knowingly disregarded the law) or two years if the discrimination was not willful. The same limitation periods apply to lawsuits related to violations of the Equal Pay Act (EPA). The limitation period begins on the date that the last discriminatory paycheck was issued. An EEOC complaint is not a precondition for such litigation. The statute of limitations is four years for employment-related disputes based on 42 U.S. Code 1981, which prohibits discrimination or harassment based on race.

In other countries, statutes of limitations for employment discrimination claims range from less than one year to six years from the date of the alleged violation or, in some countries, the date on which the employee became aware of the violation. Some countries have specific laws and statutes of limitations for claims related to unpaid wages, claims by day laborers and domestic servants, pension claims, and other employment-related matters. Some employment-related disputes—such as claims for wrongful termination, retaliatory dismissal, or workplace injuries—are covered by statutes of limitations for contract and personal injury litigation.

Intellectual Property Infringement

Many companies, not-for-profit organizations, and government agencies maintain information related to registered intellectual property, including copyrights, trademarks, patents, and industrial designs. In most countries, statutes of limitations for civil actions related to infringement of intellectual property rights range from three to six years from the date of the alleged violation. According to 17 U.S. Code 507, the statute of limitations for civil litigation related to copyright infringement is three years after the infringing act occurred. According to 35 U.S. Code 286, the statute of limitations for patent infringements is six years. U.S. law does not specify a statute of limitations for trademark infringement, but infringing acts may be covered by state laws related to fraud, consumer protection, or other matters.

The risk window for intellectual property litigation is determined by the long period of protection for copyright, trademarks, patents, and industrial designs. For written works, most countries have adopted the Berne Convention, which provides copyright protection for a minimum of 50 years following the death of the author of a work. In the United States, EU member states, Australia, and some other countries, the period of protection is 70 years after the author's death. The minimum copyright period for photographs is 25 years after the photograph was created. For cinematographic works, the minimum copyright period is 50 years after the work's creation or initial showing. In the United States, works of corporate authorship— that is, works written by an organization's employees as part of their jobs or by contractors hired for that purpose—enter the public domain 120 years after their creation or 95 years after publication, whichever occurs first.

In most countries, registered trademarks and service marks are protected for 10 years subject to indefinite renewals at 10-year intervals. Patent laws in most countries comply with the World Trade Organization's Agreement on Trade Related Aspects of Intellectual Property Rights, which protects an invention for 20 years from the date a patent application was filed. Industrial designs and databases may be protected for a shorter period.

Anticompetitive Practices

Many countries have competition laws, antitrust laws, and antimonopoly laws that prohibit anticompetitive business practices such as price collusion, predatory pricing, minimum price requirements, exclusive dealing arrangements, market division agreements among competing companies, and restricting the supply of products. In the United States, the statute of limitations for litigation related to anticompetitive activity is four years after the cause of action accrued, as specified in 15 U.S. Code 15b. In European countries, statutes of limitations range from two years to five years from the date of the violation or, in some countries, the date that the claimant becomes aware of the anticompetitive activity, subject to an absolute maximum limitation period.

Summary of Major Points

☑ Information is subject to laws and regulations in the governmental jurisdictions where it is created, collected, stored, or processed. Globally, tens of thousands of laws, regulations, standards, and guidelines contain provisions that may affect an organization's information governance policies, practices, and initiatives.

☑ All countries have laws, regulations, or other legal instruments that require organizations to create, collect, retain, and—in some cases—destroy information related to certain business activities and operations. As their principal purpose, these requirements ensure that information related to regulated activities and operations will be available for examination by auditors, investigators, inspectors, and other government officials.

☑ Data protection laws, sometimes described as data privacy laws, regulate the collection, use, and distribution of personally identifiable information by companies, government agencies, not-for-profit entities, and other organizations.

☑ Various laws and regulations specify security requirements for certain information maintained by companies, government agencies, not-for-profit entities, and other organizations. These laws and regulations require organizations to develop security plans, destroy certain information in a secure manner, prevent data breaches and notify the affected parties when breaches occur, and produce backup copies of specific information.

☑ Many countries have laws and regulations that mandate the disclosure of certain information by companies, government agencies, and not-for-profit organizations in specific circumstances. Freedom of information laws allow the public to request information from government agencies, but some laws require organizations to disclose certain information to government agencies, to data subjects, or to the public. Other laws prohibit the disclosure of information about specific matters.

☑ Civil codes define statutes of limitations for breach of contract, personal injury, property damage, anticompetitive business practices, professional malpractice, libel, and other matters. Limitation periods establish the risk window for litigation, government investigations, regulatory compliance, tax audits, and other matters that expose an organization to costly legal proceedings, tax reassessments, penalties for compliance violations, or other adverse outcomes. They also have an impact on records retention and other information-related policies and practices.

Part 3

Enabling Technologies for Information Governance

Information governance is principally concerned with policy and strategy, and it is also deeply affected by technology. In most organizations, a high percentage of information is created, maintained, and distributed by technology resources. Most information-related operations and activities have a technological component, and all information governance stakeholders utilize technology to carry out the responsibilities discussed in Part 1. Information technology creates and maintains an organization's computing and networking infrastructure, and it provides the technology to support other stakeholders. Information security uses technology to protect information from unauthorized access, disclosure, alteration, or destruction. Records management develops policies and procedures for organization, retrieval, and lifecycle management of digital content, while archival administration uses technology to preserve digital content of historical value. Data science uses technology to extract insight from voluminous digital content. The other stakeholders—compliance, risk management, and legal affairs—each use technology to support specific business operations.

Broadly defined, enabling technologies provide capabilities that support an organization's objectives and requirements. Literally, they enable the completion of tasks or activities that would otherwise be difficult or impossible to perform. The following sections survey technologies that play an enabling role in information governance initiatives. The survey is divided into four categories:

1. Technologies that organize, analyze, and categorize information.

2. Technologies that manage the information lifecycle.

3. Technologies that retrieve information.

4. Technologies that address risk management and information security requirements.

The survey defines each technology, describes its most important characteristics, and discusses its impact on information governance stakeholders and requirements. The technology impact matrix in Table 4 in Appendix D summarizes the specific technologies that affect information governance stakeholders.

The survey emphasizes technologies that information governance specialists need to know about. Some of the technologies are well established and widely implemented in companies, government agencies, and not-for-profit organizations. Others are at an earlier stage of user acceptance. The survey is limited to commercially available technologies that affect multiple information governance stakeholders and initiatives. Experimental technologies and those that support a single information governance function—the many technologies that improve the efficiency of IT operations, technologies that automate the case management process in legal departments, or data mining technologies that are used in data science projects, for example—are intentionally omitted.

Information Organization and Analysis

The following sections describe six technologies that organize, categorize, and analyze information maintained by companies, government agencies, not-for-profit entities, and other organizations:

1. Enterprise content management

2. Digital asset management

3. Physical records management software

4. File analysis software

5. Automatic document categorization

6. Master data management

7. Collaboration software

With the notable exception of physical records management software, these technologies organize and analyze digital information. Master data management organizes structured digital data. The other technologies operate on unstructured digital content.[75]

Enterprise Content Management

Enterprise content management (ECM) software creates and maintains an organized, searchable repository of digital documents and other unstructured digital content. Examples include word processing files, spreadsheets, email messages, digital images generated by document scanners or digital cameras, presentation aids, web pages, computer-aided design files, graphic arts files, blogs, audio recordings, and video recordings. Digital content of different types from a variety of sources can be comingled within a given repository, and multiple repositories can be established for specific organizational units, business processes, or content

---

[75] Imprecisely defined, unstructured digital content is not organized in a predefined manner. The phrase is often used broadly to denote any digital content other than a database or similarly organized data file.

types. Applicable standards include ISO 12651-1, *Electronic document management—Vocabulary—Part 1: Electronic document imaging*; ISO/TR 14105, *Document management—Change management for successful electronic document management system (EDMS) implementation*; ISO 16175-2, *Information and documentation—Principles and functional requirements for records in electronic office environments—Part 2: Guidelines and functional requirements for digital records management systems*; ISO 22957, *Document management—Analysis, selection and implementation of electronic document management systems (EDMS)*; and BS PAS 89:2012, *Enterprise content management: Code of practice*.

ECM is a well-established, widely implemented technology that has been commercially available for more than three decades. ECM software is available for in-house installation on servers operated by an organization's information technology unit or as a cloud-based offering. Enterprise content management systems are sometimes characterized as electronic document management systems, but ECM functionality is not limited to document organization and retrieval. Subject to product-specific variations, ECM systems also support the incorporation of digital content into web pages; version control for website content; preparation of presentation aids with media content; and management of rights and permissions for video presentations, conference call recordings, artworks, and audio-visual media. Some of these capabilities are also supported by other information governance technologies discussed in subsequent sections.

ECM software creates and maintains repositories that combine topical folders with in-depth indexing for organization and retrieval of digital content:

- *Authorized users can define hierarchically structured file plans (taxonomies) with labeled folders and subfolders nested to multiple levels.* Digital content can be imported into a designated repository by dragging and dropping it into specified folders or subfolders, by batch transfers from directories or subdirectories on network servers, or by saving it within its originating applications—a word processing document or presentation can be saved to a designated repository when it is created or edited, for example.

- *Some ECM developers offer prebuilt file taxonomies for specific industries or widely encountered business functions to simplify implementation.* Industry examples include banking and insurance, and human resources, project management, and contract management are some business functions for which prebuilt file taxonomies may be implemented. These prebuilt taxonomies can be customized for specific situations.

- *ECM applications support user-defined metadata at the folder, subfolder, and item level for indexing and descriptive purposes.* Some metadata, such as the date a folder or document was created, can be derived automatically. Other information must be key-entered when digital content enters a repository. All metadata is fully searchable. Full-text indexing can be applied to character-coded content.

- *Digital documents needed for a given purpose can be identified through a variety of browsing options.* Users may browse through folders and subfolders; search metadata associated with specific folders, subfolders, and items; or search by words or phrases contained in documents, assuming that full-text indexing is utilized. Retrieval functionality includes exact matches of specified field values, relational expressions, Boolean operators, and phrase searching (where full-text indexing is utilized).

- *Some ECM applications permit simultaneous searching of multiple repositories.* This capability, sometimes characterized as federated searching, is discussed more fully later in this part. Federated searching may be limited to repositories maintained by the ECM application or extended to other information sources such as online databases, websites, or shared files on network servers.

- *Security controls limit access to digital content on a need-to-know basis to prevent unauthorized retrieval of personally identifiable information, protected health information, or other confidential or sensitive information.* An organization can define access privileges at the repository, folder, subfolder, and item levels. Search results are limited to digital content that a user is authorized to see, and searchers are not aware of the existence of unauthorized content.

- *An ECM application maintains an audit trail of document-related activity.* It tracks all input, editing, deletion, retrieval requests, display, printing, or other actions performed by a specific user with a given digital document, including failed access attempts by unauthorized persons.

With its flexible retrieval functionality and ability to handle a broad range of digital content, ECM is an important technology for all information governance stakeholders with the possible exception of archival administration, which is responsible for permanent preservation of information of historical value. ECM is not an archiving technology. It is intended for digital content that is in the active phase of the information lifecycle. For records management, ECM is the principal technology for organization and online retrieval of digital content that is consulted regularly and frequently for business purposes. In companies, government agencies, and not-for-profit organizations, it is the technology of choice for actively referenced content with demanding retrieval requirements.

- *Retrieved content can be sent as an email attachment, uploaded to a shared workspace, or reviewed and edited by authorized persons within its originating application or a compatible equivalent.* ECM applications also allow authorized users to append comments, instructions, or free-form annotations to folders, subfolders, or items, and they will track changes and conclusively identify the latest versions of digital content. These capabilities are particularly useful for legal briefs, contracts and agreements, engineering specifications, regulatory submissions, standard operating procedures, and other documents that are subject to multiple revisions and a prescribed approval process involving multiple stakeholders.

- *Some ECM applications provide a secure collaboration space.* In this space, digital content can be saved for controlled access by approved external parties—litigation-related documents that an organization's legal department wants to share with outside counsel, for example, or technical drawings that an organization wants to share with engineering consultants.

- *Some ECM applications support workflow programming for business processes.* These processes require routing of digital content among authorized persons in a prescribed sequence in order to complete transactions or other operations.

To address compliance and risk management concerns, an organization can create an ECM repository of digital content associated with specific regulatory requirements. Similarly, ECM repositories can house digital content that is relevant for specific legal proceedings or, in the case of data science, for analytical projects. As with other enabling technologies, information technology is responsible for the computing and networking infrastructure within which ECM operates. Information security must ensure that digital content is protected against unauthorized access, data breaches, and other adverse events, and it must take appropriate action when such events occur. Compared to organization of digital content in folders on network drives or elsewhere, ECM repositories are much more secure.

Digital Asset Management

As cited in Part 1, ISO 55000, *Asset management—Overview, principles and terminology*, defines an asset as "an item, thing or entity that has potential or actual value to an organization." While the phrase "digital asset" can be broadly applied to any valuable digital content, **digital asset management (DAM)** technology has a narrower focus. DAM applications are designed for storage, cataloging, indexing, retrieval, distribution, and protection of visual and audio content. These digital assets include photographs, video recordings, logos, animation, three-dimensional models, product imagery, podcasts, and recorded music. In companies, government agencies, cultural institutions, and other organizations, visual and audio materials are important and, in some cases, revenue-generating resources that must be safeguarded and tightly controlled. They may support educational programs, marketing initiatives, or public relations campaigns, and they can be sold or licensed for authorized use.

Digital asset management is variously viewed as a standalone technology or as a focused subset of enterprise content management. The two technologies are conceptually similar. They each create and maintain a centralized repository of digital content, and they support similar functionality for storage, organization, indexing, and retrieval of digital objects and their associated metadata. Certain types of digital content, such as advertising materials or technical documents with embedded illustrations, can be effectively managed by either an ECM application or a DAM application. Some ECM products can be optionally configured with a digital asset management module, but standalone DAM applications typically offer a broader range of capabilities:

1. DAM applications can import photographs, video recordings, audio recordings, and other digital assets from various devices and media in a wide range of formats. Digital assets can be imported individually or in batches.

2. DAM applications store digital assets in a secure repository, which can be organized by asset type, by the business function to which an asset pertains, or by other categories.

3. Certain metadata can be automatically extracted from digital assets. Digital photographs, for example, typically include embedded metadata that indicates the manufacturer and model of the camera used, the date and time a photograph was taken, the focal length, the exposure time, the image resolution, the image format, the image size, and other information about the photograph.

4. Additional descriptive or indexing metadata—including copyright notices, licensing restrictions, and usage guidelines—can be key-entered into user-defined fields. Authorized users can also add titles, headlines, captions, cut-lines, annotations, special instructions, and other information about a digital asset.

5. Authorized users can search for digital assets by specified field values or by words or phrases in titles, captions, or other labels. Retrieved images can be displayed as thumbnails or in other preview formats. Collections of digital assets can be assembled for specific purposes. Digital assets can be rendered for downloading in different sizes, resolutions, and file formats to satisfy a variety of end-user requirements.

6. DAM applications can track and tabulate requests, intellectual property rights, and end-user license agreements for digital assets. Digital watermarks can be added to prevent unauthorized use of preview versions. End-user licensing agreements can be displayed for approval by the requester before a retrieved asset is downloaded.

7. DAM applications support version control, revision histories, audit trails, and other capabilities that monitor the storage and use of digital assets.

Digital asset management is an important technology for most information governance stakeholders. For records management and archival administration, DAM technology provides a reliable repository for organization, retention, and preservation of audio-visual content, a valuable and voluminous group of information resources. Centralization of digital assets in a controlled repository protects them against unauthorized access, unlicensed use, unauthorized modification, or other events that have an impact on compliance, risk management, and legal affairs. In some fields, such as healthcare and financial services, a DAM application may store marketing materials, training materials, product labels, customer communications, or other digital assets that are subject to regulatory compliance requirements.

For legal affairs, a DAM application simplifies the handling of rights and permissions, the preparation of end-user agreements, and compliance with discovery orders for digital assets. Information security must ensure that DAM repositories are protected against unauthorized access, data breaches, and other adverse events, and it must take appropriate action when such events occur. Archival administration may utilize DAM technology to preserve audio-visual content of historical value. Data science specialists may work on analytical projects that involve audio or visual information.

Physical Records Management Software

Physical records management software is designed to inventory and track paper documents as well as photographic media, computer disks and tapes, audio recording media, and video recording media. The software maintains a database that contains information about the characteristics and locations of physical records, which may be stored in file rooms, warehouses, or other repositories, either on-premises or offsite. The software may be installed on an organization's own server or accessed through a cloud-based provider. The records may be housed in filing cabinets, stored on shelves, or packed in boxes.

Physical records management software supports the following capabilities:

1. Authorized users can determine the storage locations of specific folders, boxes, or other items. System administrators can define user privileges to prevent unauthorized access to specific database records. Some products support advanced retrieval functionality such as Boolean operations, relational expressions, root word searching, wildcard characters, and full-text searching of item descriptions.

2. Library-like circulation control functionality tracks records that have been removed from storage by authorized users. Folders, boxes, or other items are typically barcoded to simplify data entry and tracking. Some products support radio-frequency identification (RFID) technology. The software will create and maintain an audit trail and circulation history for all items requested and returned to storage by authorized users.

3. Physical records management software can maintain customer-defined retention periods for specific records series and associate that information with folders, boxes, or other items in storage. The software will calculate destruction dates based on the designated retention periods. The calculated destruction dates are inserted into database records for specific items. The software can identify records with elapsed retention periods and prepare notices of impending destruction for submission to and review by authorized persons. Authorized persons can suspend destruction of records that are relevant for litigation, government investigations, audits, or other legal or quasi-legal proceedings. The software can create and maintain documentation to identify items destroyed in conformity with an organization's retention policies and schedule.

4. Physical records management software can generate a variety of preformatted and ad hoc reports, including records control sheets; transportation work orders; barcode labels; pick lists; statistical summaries of records in storage; retrieval activity reports for specific time periods, program units, or items; lists of items in circulation by program unit, date, or other parameters; lists of records destroyed by program unit; and lists of records subject to holds for litigation, audits, or other purposes.

5. Physical records management software can allocate space and track the specific storage locations of items in file rooms and warehouses. It can display a map,

listing, or other representation of the storage area that indicates available space for a given quantity of records. The software can also track items that are relocated from one location to another.

While information governance initiatives are closely associated with digital content that is maintained online, many organizations continue to maintain valuable legacy documents and other information in physical format. Among information governance stakeholders, physical records management software has a direct impact on records management and archival administration—two functions that are responsible for storing, tracking, and controlling access to paper documents and other physical records in warehouses, file rooms, and other locations. For risk management, compliance, and legal affairs, physical records management software provides effective control over documents and other information-bearing objects that may be needed for regulatory compliance, legal proceedings, government investigations, audits, or other purposes. For information security, physical records management software provides safeguards that prevent unauthorized access to paper documents and other items. It also tracks responsibility for records that have been removed from approved storage locations. For information technology, physical records management software can be used to track magnetic tapes or other media in offline storage.

File Analysis Software

File analysis software surveys and analyzes an organization's unstructured data, which is broadly defined to include word processing documents, spreadsheets, presentations, email messages, digital images, HTML files, social media content, video recordings, and audio recordings. File analysis software conducts nonintrusive surveys of designated storage repositories to collect information about the data files they contain. It provides information that cannot be easily obtained by other means.

While features and functions vary from product to product, most file analysis applications support some combination of the following capabilities:

1. Target repositories can include an organization's network drives, local drives on network-attached desktop and laptop computers, email servers, SharePoint sites and other collaboration workspaces, and ECM repositories. Some file analysis applications can also survey cloud-based storage repositories and file sharing services. The most versatile applications can identify and analyze hundreds of file formats, including obsolete formats.

2. Information collected about a data file may include, but is not necessarily limited to, the creator, the storage location, the file size, the file type, the date the file was last accessed or modified, and the existence and storage locations of duplicate copies.

3. Some file analysis applications can identify data files that contain personally identifiable information, protected health information, payment card information,

or other sensitive information. The analysis can highlight unrestricted or otherwise unsecured data files that contain sensitive information.

4. Some file analysis applications survey and evaluate user behavior. They can identify users who have accessed, modified, or copied specific data files, including files that contain sensitive information. Usage information can be reported to data file owners for review. Some file analysis applications can highlight users with excessive access privileges or suspicious access activity such as repeated unsuccessful attempts to access specific files.

File analysis generates information that supports planning, decision making, and action by information governance stakeholders. Records management can use the information to identify aged or inactive files—those files that have not been accessed since a specified date, for example, or files that have been accessed less than a specified number of times. Such files can be tagged for deletion or transfer to lower cost storage. Information collected by file analysis software can play an important role in planning for system upgrades or replacements that involve large-scale data migrations, which impact all information governance stakeholders. At a minimum, duplicate data files can be identified and excluded from migration, thereby reducing the cost of a system upgrade or replacement. Information collected by file analysis software is also useful for data center consolidation, legacy data cleanup, elimination of duplicate data files, and other storage optimization initiatives that are important for information technology, records management, and archival administration.

> Of particular significance for information security, compliance, risk management, and legal affairs, file analysis software provides information about the characteristics and use of data files with sensitive content. To reduce the risk of data breaches, information governance stakeholders can redact or restrict access to such data files. Aged, inactive, and duplicate files that contain sensitive information can be tagged for deletion or for evaluation to determine whether continued retention is warranted.

Automatic Document Categorization

Automatic document categorization, also known as *automatic text categorization* or *automatic text classification*, is a technology that assigns digital documents to predefined categories based on their contents and other characteristics. The categories may pertain to specific topics, people, organizations, clients, events, projects, or other matters. In an automatic categorization implementation, categories may be represented by electronic folders in a designated repository. Documents are assigned to appropriate folders without analysis by a subject expert or other human intervention. Alternatively, the automatic categorization process may attach subject terms or other metadata to a document. Regardless of approach, automatic categorization replaces manual filing and indexing of paper and digital documents.

Automatic categorization as an alternative to manual filing and indexing has been the subject of information science research since the 1960s, but early implementations were pilot projects of limited scope and effectiveness. The technology improved steadily through the 1990s, but commercial viability awaited the widespread availability of character-coded digital documents, which is a relatively recent development. Automatic categorization components—so-called categorization engines—are now offered by a number of software developers, and they have been incorporated into enterprise content management implementations, records management applications, email archiving systems, electronic discovery systems, and other technologies. Research is continuing, and future improvements can be expected.

An **email archiving system** is software that creates and maintains an organized, searchable repository of digital documents and other unstructured digital content.

While specific features and functions vary, automatic categorization technology has the following basic characteristics:

1. A defined framework of categories is a precondition for automatic categorization. Human intervention is required to create a framework of topical folders that reflect the subject content of documents to be categorized. Some automatic categorization engines can import an existing structure of topical folders from an ECM implementation, a records management application, an email archiving system, or another organized repository.

2. Automatic categorization operates on character-coded text—word processing files, email messages, text documents in the PDF format, HTML files, and text generated from digital document images by optical character recognition, for example. Automatic categorization can process documents in most languages, an important consideration for information governance stakeholders in multinational and transnational organizations. Automatic categorization is not intended for digital photographs or other graphic images, although it can process titles and captions associated with graphic content. Software that can automatically categorize visual content is at a precommercial stage of development.

3. As an essential first step in an automated categorization implementation, a sample of documents must be manually categorized by subject experts or other knowledgeable persons. The purpose is to teach the automatic categorization software how to categorize documents with specific characteristics. This learning phase lays the foundation for categorization decisions. The sample must be large enough to accurately represent the collection of documents to be categorized. Performance can be improved by adding documents to the sample or by manually recategorizing documents when errors are detected. Some automatic categorization engines can also benefit from examples of documents that do not match specific categories.

4. In the categorization phase, documents are processed to determine the categories to which they relate. Natural language processing, semantic analysis, and statistical models are used to generate a numerical score indicating the likelihood that a given document is associated with a specific category. Some documents may be assigned to multiple categories.

Automatic categorization is an important technology for any information governance initiative that requires systematic organization of a document collection.

Compared to manual filing and indexing, automatic document categorization is faster and more consistent, although not necessarily more accurate. It is particularly useful for electronic discovery, freedom of information requests, and other initiatives where large quantities of email messages, word processing files, and other digital documents must be categorized quickly. Among information governance stakeholders, legal affairs, compliance, and risk management are directly impacted by legally mandated discovery.

For records management and archival administration, automatic document categorization can simplify the implementation of ECM, records management applications, and digital preservation applications with large document backlogs that must be organized and indexed. In such situations, manual categorization is prohibitively labor intensive. Automatic categorization can also be used to identify documents with sensitive or offensive content and to eliminate documents with trivial content that do not warrant retention; for example, email messages that merely schedule an appointment or that confirm receipt of a message.

Master Data Management

According to the Gartner IT Glossary, master data management (MDM) is "a technology-enabled discipline in which business and IT work together to ensure the uniformity, accuracy, stewardship, semantic consistency and accounting of the enterprise's shared master data assets." Other sources present similar definitions. As defined in ISO 22745-2, *Industrial automation systems and integration—Open technical dictionaries and their application to master data—Part 2: Vocabulary*, master data is "data held by an organization that describes the entities that are both independent and fundamental for that organization and that it needs to reference in order to perform its transactions."

Master data is an authoritative collection of information that support an organization's critical business processes. Examples include, but are not limited to, information about an organization's employees, customers or constituents, products, business locations, policies, procedures, events, contracts, or financial accounts. **Master data management** is an aspect of data governance that is concerned with creating and maintaining authoritative reference data. It also establishes a unified repository of such information—a **master data hub**—as an enterprise-wide replacement for decentralized databases that are created, maintained, and utilized by specific applications. A master data hub stores records that consist of predefined data elements. Compared to other enabling technologies discussed in this book, master data management is notable for its focus on structured data rather than unstructured digital content.

Master data management is not a technology per se, but it is a technology-based information initiative. MDM software provides technical tools that enable an organization to create and maintain master data hubs. While specific features and functions vary, MDM software supports the following capabilities:

1. MDM software creates a master data hub by collecting and consolidating existing data about a specific matter. The source data is typically derived from

application-specific databases. Depending on the MDM model selected, a master data hub may store master data, or it may function as a central registry that contains links to the location of master data in external locations. In either case, a master data hub is typically limited to one category of data. Some MDM software is designed to create and maintain master data hubs for particular types of information—a customer data hub, a product data hub, a supplier data hub, or an employee data hub, for example—or for particular vertical markets such as pharmaceuticals, financial services, higher education, or public safety.

2. Data quality assurance is an important aspect of MDM. ISO 9000, *Quality management systems—Fundamentals and vocabulary*, defines quality as the "degree to which a set of inherent characteristics of an object fulfills requirements." ISO 8000-110, *Data Quality—Part 110, Master data: Exchange of characteristic data: Syntax, semantic encoding, and conformance to data specifications*, defines the fundamental characteristics of master data quality. Data quality problems are widely recognized. Critical data about customers, products, suppliers, or other matters may vary in content and format. Information maintained by application-specific databases may be out-of-date—a customer's address may have changed, for example—or be incomplete—the address may not include a nine-digit ZIP code. Multiple application-specific databases may have different billing addresses, shipping addresses, or contact persons for the same customer. Complexity increases in multinational and transnational organizations that maintain information in multiple countries and multiple languages. To address these issues, MDM implementations typically utilize data-cleaning tools that identify conflicting data, missing data elements, improperly formatted data, misspellings, inconsistent abbreviations, and other problems, some of which may be correctable without manual intervention. Some MDM software validates data against external sources such as a postal reference file or a database of standard abbreviations. Some MDM software can identify and remove duplicate data.

3. A master data hub maintains a single copy of data that authorized business processes can access. Master data is processed by multiple applications, which may modify it for their own purposes. The master data hub must be synchronized with these application-specific changes. MDM software monitors the changes and updates the master data accordingly.

4. MDM software maintains a searchable audit trail of additions, modifications, and other events that involve master data. Some MDM software allows an organization to retain historical versions of master data for comparative analysis or other purposes.

MDM is widely viewed as an aspect or extension of data governance, which, as previously noted in Part 1, is closely aligned with information governance. MDM has an obvious impact on an organization's information technology function, which must provide technical resources and expertise to create, maintain, and support master data hubs. MDM is equally important for other information governance stakeholders. Data quality, a key component of MDM, is a significant concern for compliance, risk management, and legal affairs. Inaccurate or incomplete data can compromise regulatory compliance, increase risk, and raise legal issues.

Consolidation of critical data benefits other information governance stakeholders. For records management and archival administration, a master data repository simplifies the development and implementation of enterprise-wide retention rules and preservation guidelines. For information security, a single data repository is easier to safeguard than multiple application-specific databases. For data science, a master data hub provides a unified source for information needed for analytical projects.

Collaboration Software

Collaboration software, sometimes characterized as groupware, facilitates cooperation and communication among members of teams, committees, task forces, governing boards, and other workgroups. The software creates and maintains a secure collaborative workspace for interaction and information sharing by group participants. Typically, the participants are working together on a specific project, program, legal case, event, or other business initiative, which may be open-ended or scheduled for completion within a prescribed timeframe. Collaboration software and the collaborative workspace may be implemented on an in-house server or by a cloud-based service provider. The latter approach is popular where participants are geographically dispersed or where the collaborative space will be made available to external parties.

While capabilities vary, collaboration software supports some combination of the following features and functions:

1. As a secure alternative to sharing files that are saved in folders on network drives, collaboration software can maintain a central library of documents, video recordings, graphic images, and other digital content for access by authorized participants. Digital content can be uploaded to the central library from network drives, enterprise content management systems, digital asset management systems, or other repositories.

2. Documents maintained in the central library or another designated location within the collaborative workspace can be edited by authorized participants. Version control capabilities track changes that are made to specific documents. Users can append comment tags to digital content. The final version of a document can be saved as a PDF file to prevent further editing. Some collaboration software supports workflow scripts for content approval.

3. The collaborative workspace typically includes a chat room, message board, discussion board, blog, or other components that allow authorized participants to contribute ideas or impromptu comments about specific topics. Other useful tools include project timetables, calendars to arrange group meetings, and a dashboard that summarizes recent activity and upcoming events.

4. Collaboration software supports the creation and dissemination of surveys or polls to collect participants' opinions about decisions, proposed actions, or other matters.

5. A collaborative workspace can have its own email address, a useful feature that allows external parties to send messages and documents to it directly.

As discussed in Part 1 of this book, communal pursuit of organizational interests is a principal characteristic of all governance initiatives. Because it promotes interaction, cooperation, and consultation, collaboration software is an important enabling technology for information governance. It provides an effective vehicle for dialog, consensus building, and information sharing among stakeholders, and it can be used as an information governance board to facilitate decision making and other activities.

Information Lifecycle Management

The following sections describe six technologies that manage the lifecycle of digital content:

1. Records management application software

2. Email archiving software

3. Digital preservation software

4. Website archiving

5. Social media archiving

6. File conversion software

Records Management Application Software

Records management application (RMA) software creates and maintains a reliable repository for retention of digital documents and other digital content. Designed for digital content that is in the inactive phase of the information lifecycle, RMA software complements rather than competes with the enterprise content management. Like ECM applications, RMA software uses a combination of folders and in-depth indexing to organize and retrieve digital content, but RMA software provides retention functionality that is absent from ECM applications.[76] In particular, RMA software can identify digital content that is eligible for destruction in conformity with an organization's retention policies. Applicable standards and specifications include DoD 5015.2-STD, *Electronic Records Management Software Applications Design Criteria Standard*, which was developed by the United

---

[76] To provide a complete lifecycle solution for recorded information, some developers of ECM applications offer a records management module as an optional feature. When reference activity diminishes, digital content can be transferred from an ECM repository to an RMA repository, which functions as a back-end retention component.

States Department of Defense;[77] *MoReq2010: Modular Requirements for Records Systems—Volume 1: Core Services & Plug-in Modules*, issued by the DLM Forum, a not-for-profit organization established in 1994 by the European Commission; and the Victorian Electronic Records Strategy (VERS) Standard PROS 99/007, *Management of Electronic Records*, issued by the Public Record Office Victoria.

An RMA repository is organized into folders and subfolders that correspond to categories in a user-defined file plan. RMA repositories can import digital content in a variety of file formats. Digital content can also be transferred to the repository from office productivity software, email systems, CAD programs, imaging software, workgroup collaboration software, or other originating applications. Depending on the method employed, an RMA repository may store the digital content, or it may store links to word processing files, PDF files, email messages, spreadsheets, or other digital items that are located elsewhere—on a network file server, for example.

Regardless of input source or storage method, retention functionality is RMA software's distinctive characteristic:

- **Retention periods.** Authorized users can specify retention periods for digital content in conformity with an organization's approved retention policies and schedules. Retention periods may be specified at the folder, subfolder, or item level. Retention periods may be based on elapsed time or designated events such as termination of a contract or completion of a project.

- **Official copies.** Digital content transferred to an RMA repository is considered the official copy for reference and retention purposes. It cannot be edited, deleted, or replaced until its designated retention period elapses. Revised content added to a closed file is treated as a unique record rather than as a replacement for older versions.

- **Destruction lists.** Even then, destruction of digital content is not automatic: RMA software generates lists of digital content that is eligible for destruction on a specified date. The list is submitted to designated persons for approval before destruction is executed.

- **Unauthorized destruction safeguards.** RMA software provides safeguards against the unauthorized destruction of electronic records by issuing a warning when such destruction is attempted. An audit trail tracks all activity involving specific digital content.

- **Destruction documentation.** RMA software can print certificates of destruction or other documentation for digital content that was destroyed in conformity with an organization's retention policies and schedules.

---

[77] The National Archives and Records Administration has endorsed DoD 5015.2-STD for use by U.S. government agencies when selecting RMA software to store electronic records as official copies and to facilitate the transfer of permanent electronic records to the National Archives. It is not a national or international standard, but DoD 5015.2-STD provides useful criteria for evaluation and selection of RMA products by companies, not-for-profit organizations, and other entities.

- **Retention status.** Some RMA products can also track the retention status of paper and photographic records stored in file rooms or offsite locations, but RMA technology was specifically developed for digital content.

- **Content review.** Retrieved content is displayed by launching its originating application. If the originating application has been replaced or is otherwise unavailable, viewing modules can display digital content in a variety of file formats, including obsolete formats.

For records management, RMA software is the principal enabling technology for lifecycle management of digital content. Like other enabling technologies, RMA software may be implemented in-house on a server operated by an organization's information technology unit or as a cloud-based application supervised by IT. In either case, IT's involvement is required for technical support. Among other information governance stakeholders, information security must ensure that an RMA repository is properly protected against unauthorized access, data breaches or other adverse events, and it must take appropriate action when such events occur.

RMA software addresses compliance and risk management concerns about premature or inadvertent destruction of digital content that is subject to legally mandated retention requirements. For legal affairs, RMA software can provide a repository for preservation of information that is relevant for litigation, government investigations, or other legal proceedings. To address evidentiary requirements, RMA software can suspend destruction of selected digital content until legal proceedings are completed and all outstanding issues are resolved. Data science may access RMA repositories to obtain digital content needed for analytical projects. While an RMA repository supports permanent retention of digital content, archival administration may be better served by applications intended specifically for preservation of information.

Email Archiving Software

Email archiving software creates and maintains a reliable repository for retention of messages and their associated attachments transferred from an organization's email system. Archived messages and attachments remain in the repository until their retention periods elapse and will be deleted thereafter unless they are identified as relevant for litigation, government investigations, or other legal proceedings.

While specific characteristics and capabilities vary, most email archiving software supports some combination of the following features and functions:

1. An email repository creates and maintains an archive mailbox for each active mailbox that exists on designated email servers. The owner of the active mailbox is the owner of its archive counterpart. Any folders and subfolders established in an active mailbox will be replicated in the archive mailbox.

2. Messages are retained in mailboxes on email servers for a specified period of time, after which they are transferred to the corresponding archive mailboxes in the repository where they will be stored until their retention periods

elapse or they are otherwise deleted as permitted by an organization's retention guidelines.

3. Message archiving is performed automatically at specified intervals. Transfer of messages from email servers to archive mailboxes may be based on the age of a message or on the amount of free space in a given mailbox. Alternatively, mailbox owners may be permitted to archive messages manually.

4. Archived messages and attachments remain accessible online by mailbox owners or other authorized persons. Access privileges are typically synchronized with the mailbox from which the messages and attachments were archived. Email archiving software supports various levels of indexing, ranging from predefined index fields to full-text indexing of messages and attachments.

5. Retention periods can be based on the date that a message was sent or received or the date that it was transferred to the email archiving repository.

6. To ensure that they are preserved, copies of such messages can be transferred to a separate repository for preservation until the matters to which they pertain are fully resolved.

7. To reduce total storage requirements, some email archiving software combines data compression with single-instance storage when archiving duplicate copies of messages. Removal of duplicate messages prior to archiving is consequently unnecessary.

8. Email archiving software can generate reports and graphs about email activity in aggregate or for individual mailboxes.

Given the pervasiveness of email, email archiving software is an important technology for all information governance stakeholders. For records management and, to a less extent, archival administration, email archiving software is the principal enabling technology for retention and preservation of email. It is generally more convenient and effective than RMA software for that purpose.[78] As one of its strongest business justifications, email archiving software addresses significant compliance and risk management concerns. When combined with comprehensive policy guidance, it will ensure that messages and attachments are retained for the periods of time required to satisfy all legal and regulatory requirements to which specific messages and attachments are subject.

To simplify legal discovery and compliance with freedom of information laws, email archiving software aggregates messages and attachments into organized,

---

[78] Email archiving software is not a replacement for RMA software, which is intended for a broader range of digital content. Unlike RMA software, an email archiving repository cannot accommodate retention periods based on designated events, such as the termination of a project, and it does not support version control or provide multiformat viewing software for attachments where the originating application is not available. Generally, these shortcomings are less significant for email than for other types of digital documents. Email messages are rarely subject to version control, for example, and as long as email client software is available, users have little need for a multiformat document viewer to read messages.

searchable repositories, eliminating the need to search all network and local drives for messages that come within the scope of a subpoena or freedom of information request. Copies of relevant messages and attachments can be transferred to a separate repository for preservation until the matters to which they pertain are fully resolved.

For an organization's IT unit, transfer of messages and attachments to an email archiving product will improve the performance of email servers and clients without sacrificing convenient access to information. For information security, an email archiving repository can simplify protection of messages and attachments against unauthorized access or other adverse events. For data science, an email archiving repository may contain digital content that is needed for analytical projects.

Digital Preservation Software

Digital preservation is technology that ensures long-term integrity and usability of digital documents and other unstructured digital content of permanent value. Digital preservation software is designed for digital documents and other unstructured digital content of permanent value. Applicable standards are ISO 14721, *Space Data and Information Transfer Systems—Open Archival Information System (OAIS)—Reference Model*, which provides a framework and functional model for long-term preservation and accessibility of electronic records; ISO 18492, *Long-term preservation of electronic document-based information*, which provides methodological guidance for preservation of digital documents; ISO 16363, *Space data and information transfer systems—Audit and certification of trustworthy digital repositories*; and ISO 16919, *Space data and information transfer systems—Requirements for bodies providing audit and certification of candidate trustworthy digital repositories*. Most installations of digital preservation software are in government agencies, universities, cultural institutions, and not-for-profit organizations with archival units that are dedicated to permanent preservation of scholarly resources.[79]

Digital preservation software creates and maintains a trusted repository that provides reliable, long-term access to and usability of digital content. Digital preservation applications that comply with the Open Archival Information System (OAIS) reference model support the following features and functions:

- **Submission information package (SIP).** Digital content and associated metadata can be imported and ingested from various sources in a wide range of file formats. The imported content is described as a submission information package (SIP). A submission information package may be uploaded to a digital preservation application from a local repository, such as shared files on a network drive or an enterprise content management, or from an external entity such as a

---

[79] This discussion is limited to applications that provide a complete digital preservation solution. It excludes products intended for a specific purpose such as accessioning digital documents, checking for errors in digital content, describing and cataloging of digital content, or publishing archival finding aids for digital content online.

commercial information publisher. As part of the ingest process, digital content is checked for data corruption, viruses, or other problems.

- **Archival information package (AIP).** Archived content is assigned to an appropriate medium for long term storage. The stored content is described as an archival information package (AIP). A digital preservation application is designed to protect archived content from loss or damage that will impair its long-term accessibility and usability.

- **Dissemination information package (DIP).** Organizations can define and implement access policies and privileges for specific users or groups of users. Policies and privileges can be changed as circumstances warrant. Digital content can be accessed by various client applications, including web browsers. Archived content that is retrieved by an authorized user is described as a dissemination information package (DIP). Designated users can be limited to read-only access.

- **Format conversions.** Some digital preservation applications monitor archived content for continued usability and issue alerts when format conversions or other interventions are required. Some applications can convert digital content to file formats, such as PDF/A, that are intended for archival preservation. This conversion may be done when digital content is ingested by a digital preservation application or at a later time.

Digital preservation software differs from other lifecycle management applications in its exclusive emphasis on permanent preservation. It is not suitable for digital content with defined destruction dates. Among information governance stakeholders, digital preservation software is most significant for archival administration, but it is also an important resource for records management, which must identify permanent records when preparing retention schedules. Digital preservation technology can supplement the records management functionality provided by RMA software previously described.[80]

When implemented in-house, a digital preservation application is typically installed on a server operated by an organization's information technology unit. Cloud-based implementations also require information technology involvement to upload digital content and support locally installed client software. Information security must deal with unauthorized access, data breaches, or other incidents that involve content maintained in a digital preservation repository. Digital preservation software is not an enabling technology for compliance, risk management, and legal affairs. Those information governance stakeholders are rarely involved in historical preservation of digital content. Data science may access a digital preservation repository for information that is relevant to specific analytical projects.

---

[80] While it is intended for records management not archival administration, RMA software is compatible with some aspects of the OAIS reference model for digital preservation. RMA software can ingest digital content from various sources. It supports mechanisms to prevent deletion or modification of archival content. It allows implementing organizations to define policies and privileges for accessibility and usability of digital content by a designated user community.

Web Archiving

Web archiving technology collects and preserves the content and appearance of websites on the public Internet or organizational intranets. Website content and associated metadata is collected or "harvested" by crawler software, which visits specified websites on a predetermined schedule. The captured information is transferred to a designated repository from which it can be displayed as it appeared on the source site at the time it was captured. Web archiving technology creates and maintains a working replica of each harvested site. With some web archiving applications, crawler software can also collect information from specified websites on an organization's intranet.

Website archiving technology is available as software for on-premises implementation or as a cloud-based offering. In either case, the technology supports the following capabilities:

- *Authorized users specify the websites or domains to be crawled.* Crawler software visits each target site and navigates through it by following links. The crawler captures all website content and associated metadata. The most capable crawler software can capture challenging content such as drop-down lists, pop-up information, or other components that are activated by interaction with a given site. Where website content is subject to frequent changes, completeness of capture depends on crawling frequency.

- *Authorized users specify the timeframe for website crawling and the frequency of repeated visits to a given site.* Crawling can be time consuming, and it increases site activity, which may have an adverse impact on a site's performance. Consequently, organizations may prefer to schedule crawling during overnight hours when public access to a given site may be lower. With some web archiving applications, authorized users can specify a window of time during which crawling must be completed.

- *Captured content is stored in the WARC (Web ARChive) format, which was developed by the International Internet Preservation Consortium (IIPC).* The applicable standard is ISO 28500, *Information and documentation—WARC file format.* WARC has replaced the ARC file format, formerly used by the Internet Archive, as well as proprietary file formats for preservation of web content. WARC requires the preservation of web content and associated metadata in its exact native format. The captured site must be identical to the target site at the time it was captured, including working links, media items, attached documents, and other content.

- *Some web archiving applications will automatically delete duplicate content.* To minimize storage requirements, duplicate content that is collected during repeated visits to an unchanged site may be automatically deleted.

- *Some web archiving applications create a PDF snapshot of each web page at the time that it is captured.* To complement the WARC file, the PDF version can be exported to an external repository or to satisfy requests for website content in connection with regulatory investigations, litigation, freedom of information law inquiries, or other matters.

- *Some web archiving applications can perform transaction archiving.* They capture all browser-server interactions for a given site. Some applications can capture a user's experience of websites where content varies with the user's geographic location.

Historically, the user community for web archiving technology has been dominated by research libraries and cultural institutions that want to collect and preserve web content for future scholarly use. Those organizations developed the standards and specifications on which web archiving technology is based. Among information governance stakeholders, web archiving technology is obviously important for archival administration, but—given the increasing amount of information that is created and maintained exclusively on websites—it is also a useful resource for business purposes. In particular, it provides a reliable method of capturing and preserving website content that is relevant for regulatory compliance, litigation, or government investigations. Because website archiving software maintains the authenticity and integrity of captured content and creates a working replica of a target website, it reduces the risk that web-based information will be unavailable or unusable when requested by regulatory authorities, court-ordered discovery, or freedom of information inquiries.

Social Media Archiving

Social media archiving technology collects, indexes, and saves information that an organization posts on publicly accessible social media sites. For lifecycle management, social media archiving offers an alternative to in-place preservation of social media content. Organizations that post content on social media sites may have dozens or hundreds of user accounts, and they have limited control over preservation of posted information. Retention policies are set by site operators, and organizations must rely on a site's security provisions to prevent unauthorized modification or deletion of content.

Social media archiving technology is available as software for on-premises implementation as a cloud-based service or, less commonly, by an organization's information technology unit. For security reasons, some organizations prefer the cloud-based approach because it maintains a separation between in-house information technology resources and publicly accessible social media sites. Regardless of implementation method, social media archiving technology combines lifecycle management capabilities with other useful features and functions:

- *Social media archiving platforms capture content by monitoring specific sites on a regular schedule.* For real-time updating, some platforms monitor sites continuously. Specific sites can also be polled on demand. Capture can include content posted by an organization or content posted by others about an organization.

- *The most versatile social media archiving platforms capture and store information from a variety of social media sites.* Some social media archiving platforms are limited to specific content types—websites, for example. Social media sites that organizations may choose to archive include social networking sites such as Facebook and Google+; microblogging sites such as Twitter and Tumblr; multimedia sharing sites such as YouTube, Vimeo, Instagram, Pinterest, and Flickr; business networking sites such as LinkedIn, Xing, Yammer, IBM Connections, Salesforce Chatter; and social news sites such as Reddit, Fark, and Slashdot.

- *Captured content is stored in a single repository, but it is typically separated by type.* Some social media archiving platforms provide an enterprise search capability that enables a single retrieval operation to locate content from multiple sources. Some platforms can combine social media archiving with content from email systems, instant messaging systems, and other in-house applications.

- *Social media content and its associated metadata are preserved in its original format.* Content can be displayed as it appeared on the site from which it was archived. Hash values, time stamping, and other techniques are used to authenticate and document a chain of custody for social media content and metadata.

- *Cloud-based services can export archived content in various formats.* Archived content may be transferred to a customer-operated server, to a different cloud-based repository, or to a different social media site.

- *Some social media platforms control posting of information and access to social media sites in addition to capturing and storing content.* They can block specific features, prohibit access to certain sites from office locations, and limit posts to pre-approved content that is scanned for problematic words or phrases. Some platforms can also intercept content and route it to designated persons for manual review prior to posting.

Social media archiving is a potentially important technology for most information governance stakeholders. For records management and archival administration, social media archiving provides an effective mechanism for retention and preservation of information that is not easily handled by other lifecycle management technologies. The information security function benefits from features that require pre-approval of social media posts as well as the creation of a secure repository for archived social media content. For legal affairs, compliance, and risk management, social media archiving technology can manage content that is subject to regulatory retention mandates. It collects, indexes, and saves information that an organization posts on publicly accessible social media sites. It can also detect social media posts that pose reputational risks and identify and preserve content that is relevant for legal proceedings.

Social media content is subject to court-ordered discovery—colloquially characterized as "social" discovery—in criminal and civil litigation, including cases involving personal injury, fraudulent advertising, trademark and copyright infringement, breach of contract, defamation, and employment matters. As evidence, social media content is subject to the same preservation obligations and spoliation risks as other types of recorded information. Some social media platforms can record archived content on nonerasable media to comply with 17 CFR 17a-4(f), 17 CFR 1.31(b), and other regulations with special storage requirements. For government agencies, social media archiving technology can facilitate compliance with freedom of information requests that involve social media content.

File Conversion Software

File conversion is the process of transforming digital content from one file format to another through the use of file conversion software. As a lifecycle management technology, file conversion supports digital continuity; that is, it preserves the readability of digital content over time. File conversion is often required when an application that created digital content is replaced or discontinued. File conversion software can also be used for file sharing where the sending and receiving parties have different software.

File conversion software is available for installation and operation on in-house servers or as a cloud-based service. In either case, a source file—the file to be converted—is read, processed, and transformed into a specified target file. The following features and functions are typical:

- *While capabilities vary from product to product, file conversion applications can process a variety of file formats.* Databases, word processing documents, spreadsheets, presentations, document images, digital photographs, computer-aided design files, geo-reference files, audio recordings, and video recordings may be converted using file conversion software.

- *File conversion applications can accept source files containing computer data, audio recordings, or video recordings in a varied range of formats.* The most versatile products can read and convert over 100 file formats, including many formats that are discontinued or rarely encountered.

- *Most file conversion applications produce target files in a narrower range of widely encountered formats.* Organizations may find little need to convert files to obsolete or proprietary formats. Common format choices are PDF or PDF/A for digital documents, JPG for digital photographs, MP3 for audio recordings, and MP4 for video recording. A database is typically converted into the file format required by a specific database application. This process is usually done in the context of a database upgrade or replacement—from Oracle to SQL Server, for example.

- *Files can be converted individually or in batches.* Batch conversion, a potentially time-consuming process that can be scheduled to run during off-hours, is the most practical approach for software upgrades or replacement involving voluminous digital content. On-demand conversion of individual files is useful for file sharing. With some file conversion software, a shortcut can be added to the menu bar of applications that produce digital documents or other source files.

- *Full file conversion preserves all content of the source file, including metadata, embedded objects, hyperlinks, and macros or scripts, which is usually the preferred approach for lifecycle management of digital content.* For other purposes, some file conversion applications can alter a source file—producing a digital image from a word processing file, converting a color photograph to a grayscale image, or splitting a single PDF file into multiple pages, for example.

- *File conversion software may preserve a copy of the original source file.* This practice allows reversion to the original if a problem occurs with the target file.

As a lifecycle management tool, file conversion software is an important enabling technology for records management and archival administration, two information governance stakeholders that are responsible for retention and preservation of digital content. Multiple iterations of file conversion may be required to satisfy multidecade retention or permanent preservation requirements. For compliance and risk management, file conversion software can satisfy electronic recordkeeping laws and regulations that mandate the continued readability of digital content throughout its retention period.

Information Retrieval

The following sections discuss four technologies that offer special information retrieval capabilities:

1. Full-text indexing and searching

2. Federated searching

3. Predictive coding

4. E-discovery software

Full-text Indexing and Searching

Full-text indexing is a computerized indexing method for word processing files, PDF files, email messages, web pages, and other digital documents or document surrogates such as abstracts, summaries, and annotations. Full-text searching can locate documents or portions of documents that contain specific words or phrases. Full-text indexing and searching operate on character-coded digital content. They are not applicable to CAD files, audio files, video files, or other nontextual information. Full-text indexing is not applicable to digital document images unless optical character recognition is used to convert their contents to character-coded text.

Full-text indexing and searching is available as a standalone application or as components embedded in other technologies such as electronic content management. Full-text indexing and search technology is also incorporated into web search engines, its most widely encountered use. Regardless of implementation, the following capabilities are typically supported:

- **Identifying words for inclusion in an inverted index.** Full-text indexing software identifies words that documents contain and extracts them for inclusion in an inverted index—a computer file that lists words with pointers to the digital documents in which they appear. Some inverted indexes merely list the documents that contain specific words; others indicate the exact location(s) of a word within a document.

- **Identifying words not included when indexing.** Certain words are typically excluded from the indexing process. These words include prepositions, conjunctions, interjections, adverbs, and certain adjectives that rarely convey subject content. The excluded words, known as "stop words" or "noise words," are stored in a file called a "stop list," which the indexing program matches against the words encountered in a digital document.

- **Adding or deleting words.** To address special application requirements, some full-text indexing programs allow users to add words to or delete words from a stop list. However, some application planners argue against this practice, noting that the inclusion of irrelevant nouns, verbs, or adjectives as index terms increases the size of the index but has no negative impact on retrieval performance.

- **Locating specific words or phrases.** Search commands may include relational expressions, Boolean operators, or wildcard symbols. With some full-text indexing software, proximity commands allow a searcher to specify the number of permissible intervening words between two search terms and/or the sequence in which the two terms appear. With some proximity commands, a searcher can specify that two terms appear in the same line, sentence, paragraph, or page within a digital document.

- **Locating documents containing limited relevance to a specific topic.** Most nouns and verbs become searchable index terms, which results in high recall but characteristically low precision. Full-text searches can locate documents that treat specific topics peripherally, but they often retrieve many irrelevant documents.

The subject of five decades of research and development, full-text indexing and searching is now a commonplace technology. The ability to retrieve documents by the words or phrases they contain is a useful capability for all information governance stakeholders. Automatic derivation of index terms from digital documents is much faster and less expensive than manual indexing, which is an intellectually demanding, time-consuming, and labor-intensive activity.

- **Browsing terms through various searching techniques.** Less common retrieval capabilities include index browsing to facilitate term selection, case-sensitive searches, automatic searches for synonymous or related terms based on an online thesaurus, conflation operators that automatically match different verb tenses or related forms of nouns, proximity searches for words that appear between two specified words, and quorum searching to locate documents that contain a specified number of listed terms such as any three search terms from a list of seven.

- **Producing a list of digital documents based on specific retrieval parameters.** Depending on the program, the list may be sorted chronologically, by specified fields, or by relevance, based on term weighting or statistical analysis of document content. Any listed document can be selected for a complete display with search terms highlighted. Alternatively, some programs will display short document segments that contain search terms surrounded by several lines of context.

For records management, which is responsible for planning and implementing document retrieval systems, full-text indexing is often the only practical approach where a large document collection must be indexed quickly at low cost. For legal affairs, full-text indexing and searching are important components of litigation support and electronic discovery applications. For archival administration, full-text indexing and searching provide access to digital collections of historical documents.

Federated Searching

With conventional information retrieval, a search query operates on content in a single repository—records in an application-specific database, messages and attachments on an email server, or web pages on an organizational intranet, for example. **Federated search** technology, also known as *enterprise search*, performs retrieval operations on multiple content repositories simultaneously. It simplifies retrieval operations by providing a single point of access to dispersed content. Federated search technology was initially developed in the 1980s for library retrieval operations involving public access catalogs and bibliographic databases maintained by multiple providers. The applicable standard is ISO 23950, *Information and documentation—Information retrieval (Z39.50)—Application service definition and protocol specification*. In recent years, the market for federated searching has broadened to encompass nonlibrary usage scenarios and business requirements. As the number and variety of content sources has increased, federated search technology offers a fast, efficient approach for information retrieval operations that require comprehensive coverage of multiple repositories.

Federated searching may be implemented as a standalone technology for on-premises installation or cloud-based access. Alternatively, federated search functionality can be incorporated into other information retrieval platforms, such as enterprise content management or email archiving systems, to provide access to searchable content outside an application-specific repository. Whatever the configuration, federated search technology supports the following capabilities:

- *Federated searches can encompass structured or unstructured information.* Searchable content repositories can be internal or external. A federated search for information about a given customer, for example, might retrieve content from accounting and contract management databases, a master data hub, shared folders or collaboration sites that contain proposals and customer presentations, email servers, employee calendars, a project management application, and a customer relationship management system, as well as from Internet web pages, social media networks, and business databases maintained by financial services companies, credit rating companies, information aggregators, publishers, libraries, and other external providers.

- *Some federated search applications create and maintain a unified index to multiple content sources.* Other applications formulate a search query and pass it in an appropriate format to individual content sources, which have their own indexes. Federated search platforms differ in the specific content sources that they can index and search.

- *Most federated search platforms support a broad range of retrieval functionality.* These functions include Boolean operations, root word searching, phrase searching, proximity searching, synonym searching, saved searches, and the ability to limit search results by date, language, or other parameters. Search interfaces can be customized for specific user groups. Some federated search platforms support automatic completion of search queries, a feature that has proven popular with web search engines.

- *Access to some repositories and documents can be limited.* Access to specific repositories and individual documents or other content items within a repository is determined by predefined user privileges, which can be specified or denied for individuals or groups.

- *Search results may be displayed individually for each content source or consolidated to interleave results from multiple sources and remove duplicates.* Search results are limited to information that a user is authorized to access.

- *Federated search software can perform individual and specific tasks.* It can track user actions, maintain audit trails, and generate access, retrieval, and performance metrics for specific resources and individual users.

Federated search is an enabling technology for any information governance initiative that requires comprehensive retrieval functionality. As such, it has an impact on all information governance stakeholders. Compared to separately searching individual content sources, federated searching increases the likelihood that relevant content will be retrieved. For legal affairs, federated searching offers significant advantages for early case assessment, court-ordered discovery, and trial preparation where large quantities of potentially relevant documents and other evidence are dispersed in multiple repositories. It can also be used to identify digital content that comes within the scope of a litigation hold. For compliance and risk management, federated searching of multiple repositories can identify documents that may contain personally identifiable information, protected health information, or other sensitive or problematic information. For data science, federated searching can locate digital content that is relevant for analytical projects.

Predictive Coding

Predictive coding technology combines linguistic analysis with statistical calculations to identify digital documents that satisfy specific retrieval requirements. In its most widely publicized use, predictive coding provides an automated alternative to manual review of documents for court-ordered discovery for legal proceedings. Predictive coding algorithms estimate (predict) the likelihood that a given document comes within the scope of a discovery order and identifies those that appear to be relevant. According to a 2012 study by the RAND Institute for Civil Justice,[81] document review accounts for 73 percent of the cost of electronic discovery for civil litigation. As its principal benefit, technology-assisted review to identify relevant documents is faster and less expensive than traditional human review, and some studies indicate that it is at least as accurate. Where a very large quantity of documents must be reviewed, predictive coding may be the only method of complying with a discovery order in a reasonable timeframe. In addition to retrieving potentially relevant documents, predictive coding can also identify documents that are subject to attorney-client privilege.

Predictive coding is not entirely automatic. Predictive coding software must be trained to identify relevant documents. Significant human intervention is required during the training phase of the review process:

- *A sample of relevant documents—the so-called seed set or control set—must be assembled.* The relevant documents are selected by subject matter experts based on manual review of the contents or other characteristics of each document— the type of document, the date that it was created, or the author or recipient, for example. For review purposes, subject matter experts must formulate a list of words or phrases that a relevant document is likely to contain.

- *With the seed set as a model, predictive coding software reviews a test group of documents.* Using linguistic and statistical analysis, the predictive coding algorithm calculates a numerical score for each document. The result is compared to a predetermined threshold score that relevant documents must exceed.

- *Documents identified as relevant are examined by subject matter experts to evaluate the coding algorithm's effectiveness.* If necessary, additional relevant documents can be added to the seed set and the training process repeated. The seed set can be augmented during the operational phase of the review process as new relevant documents are identified.

- *Predictive coding uses various techniques to improve performance.* Concept clustering can identify documents that contain specified combinations of words. Contextual search considers the location and frequency of search terms within a document. Searches can be limited to metadata. Some predictive coding algorithms can search for synonymous terms. Predictive coding can also identify duplicate and near-duplicate documents.

As an enabling technology, predictive coding has a direct impact on legal affairs, compliance, and risk management—three disciplines that are affected by court-ordered discovery. Legal affairs and risk management can also use predictive coding for early case assessment to estimate the likely time cost of discovery in a specific

---

[81] Nicholas M. Pace and Laura Zakaras, "Where the Money Goes: Understanding Litigant Expenditures for Producing Electronic Discovery." Santa Monica, CA: RAND Corporation, 2012. *http://www.rand.org/content/dam/rand/pubs/monographs/2012/RAND_MG1208.pdf.*

legal proceeding. Apart from court-ordered discovery, predictive coding can identify documents that are relevant for internal investigations, freedom of information requests, and analytical projects, as well as documents that contain personally identifiable information, protected health information, payment card information, or other sensitive information that requires special safeguards or other attention by the information security function.

In its use of statistical models, predictive coding resembles and is sometimes confused with automatic categorization. Both technologies are limited to word processing documents, email messages, and other character-coded digital content. They cannot be applied to photographs, graphics, video recordings, audio recordings, or other nontextual items.

Both automatic categorization and predictive coding require a training phase with significant human intervention, but the two technologies have different purposes. Automatic categorization is designed to organize a document collection. Predictive coding is a retrieval technology. It searches a document collection to find items that have specific attributes. While automatic categorization is concerned with all documents in a given collection, predictive coding is exclusively concerned with identifying relevant documents. It ignores those documents that do not satisfy the specified search criteria. As another point of difference, predictive coding errors expose an organization to an accusation of deliberately failing to disclose evidence in response to a discovery order. Automatic categorization errors do not pose a comparable legal risk.

E-Discovery Software

According to The Sedona Conference®, a nonprofit research and educational organization dedicated to the study of law and policy, e-discovery is "the process of identifying, locating, preserving, collecting, reviewing, and producing Electronically Stored Information (ESI) in the context of the legal process." [82] The same aspects of e-discovery are included in definitions provided by the Grossman-Cormack Glossary of Technology-Assisted Review,[83] a widely cited legal resource, and ISO/IEC 27050-1, *Information technology—Security techniques—Electronic discovery—Part 1: Overview and concepts*. The Electronic Discovery Reference Model (EDRM) provides a detailed workflow for the e-discovery process from identification through collection, review, and production.[84]

As its name implies, e-discovery software supports the electronic discovery process by facilitating the identification, collection, review, preservation, and production of digital content that is relevant for litigation, government investigations,

---

[82] *The Sedona Conference® Glossary: E-Discovery and Digital Information Management* (Fourth Edition). April 2014 Version. Phoenix, AZ: The Sedona Conference®, 2014. *https://thesedonaconference.org/publication/The%20Sedona%20Conference®%20Glossary*.

[83] M. R. Grossman and G. V. Cormack, "Grossman-Cormack Glossary of Technology-Assisted Review," *Federal Courts Law Review*, Vol. 7, Issue 1 (2013), pp. 1-34.

[84] *http://www.edrm.net/resources/edrm-stages-explained*.

or other legal proceedings. E-discovery software may be installed on-premises or operated by a cloud-based provider. In either case, typical capabilities include the following:

- *A data collection engine identifies and retrieves potentially relevant content from multiple sources.* These sources include network drives, email servers, desktop computers, and mobile devices, as well as electronic content management systems, records management applications, email archiving systems, collaboration servers, and other repositories. The data collection engine documents the chain of custody by identifying the devices or repositories from which digital content was retrieved.

- *Keywords, dates, or other search terms are used to locate data that satisfies specified criteria.* Users can test and refine search criteria prior to collection. Collected items are transferred to a specified repository for review. The repository may be maintained on a network drive or by an electronic content management or records management application.

- *To reduce the number of files that must be reviewed, e-discovery software can identify and eliminate duplicate and near-duplicates digital content.* It can also identify and eliminate operating system files, applications, screen savers, and other items that are not relevant for legal proceedings. This process, sometimes described as "deNISTing," is based on a reference data set of unimportant system files issued by the National Software Reference Library, a project of the National Institute of Standards and Technology.

- *Digital content can be delivered to several constituencies and in multiple formats.* Digital content may be delivered to external counsel, litigants, regulatory agencies, or others in a choice of file formats.

- *Some e-discovery products also include a legal hold component that tracks the progress of preservation notices and custodian responses.* Alternatively, legal holds may be managed by a standalone application. In either case, the legal hold component maintains a repository for notifications, custodian questionnaires, confirmations, clarifications, reminders, and other documentation related to the legal hold process. Legal hold notices can be prepared from a customizable library of templates.

E-discovery has been closely associated with information governance for more than 10 years. A number of law firms, litigation support companies, and software developers have formed information governance groups to address the requirements of legal affairs, risk management, and compliance—the three stakeholders that are directly affected by e-discovery requirements. E-discovery also has an impact on records management, which often participates in the identification of data custodians who have potentially relevant digital content.

As a related technology, freedom of information response software facilitates the processing of requests to access public records under freedom of information laws.

The software aggregates the collection of freedom of information requests that are received by mail, email, phone, fax, or online submission. It routes the requests to an appropriate employee for review and response. Authorized users can search multiple repositories for responsive content. Freedom of information software includes customizable templates for confirmations, responses, and other communications. Digital content can be redacted to remove confidential information prior to response.

Risk Management and Information Security

The following sections discuss technologies that deal with key aspects of risk management and information security:

- GRC software
- Sensitive data finders
- Data anonymization software
- Data encryption software
- Data destruction technology

GRC Software

Governance, risk management, and compliance (GRC) software is the collective name for a group of computer applications that support risk management, which is broadly defined to encompass all types of strategic and operational risks, including data breaches, intellectual property infringement, and other information-related risks. Intended for organizations that want an enterprise-wide risk management framework, GRC software provides a consistent approach and central focal point for identification, assessment, tracking, and mitigation of risks. Governance, in this context, refers to the process by which an organization manages risk. The compliance aspect recognizes the impact of regulatory compliance, or the failure to comply, on an organization's risk exposure.

Available for on-premises installation or as a cloud-based application, most GRC applications consist of multiple modules that support some combination of the following features and functions:

- **Risk management.** As a core risk management component, GRC software creates and maintains a centralized registry that identifies and categorizes risks. To facilitate risk identification, some GRC applications have preformulated lists of common and unusual risks from which an organization can select those risks that are relevant to its operations and activities. Tailored lists are available for specific industries such as financial services, healthcare, and pharmaceuticals.

- **Risk assessment.** A risk assessment tool helps risk managers and other stakeholders analyze and prioritize specific risks. This tool steps users through the evaluation process for adverse events, the threats that may cause those events, the consequences of the events, the likelihood of occurrence of the events, and factors that adversely impact an organization's ability to control or recover from the events.

- **Risk response.** A risk response component tracks the progress of risk management initiatives, including investigations and audits. It identifies the roles and responsibilities of specific business units and issues alerts to remind the responsible parties when tasks need to be completed. Most GRC software uses a combination of graphs, heat maps, scorecards, and executive dashboards to monitor the status of specific risk-related activities.

- **Incident management.** An incident management component maintains a central repository of information about adverse events that require investigation or other action. Some GRC applications have prebuilt templates that standardize the types of information maintained about specific types of incidents such as data breaches, destructive weather, or regulatory noncompliance.

- **Documentation.** A documentation component stores, updates, and manages the review and approval process for several organizational documents. These documents include risk management policies, risk mitigation plans, and risk recovery procedures, as well as audit reports, incident reports, investigation reports, and other risk-related documents. Some GRC applications have a library of prewritten risk management policies, procedures, plans, and guidelines that can be edited and customized for specific situations. Some GRC applications can link to content stored in external repositories.

- **Compliance.** A compliance component maintains a repository of laws and regulations. These laws and regulations include citations, interpretations, effective dates, the business processes affected, and the employees who are principally responsible for compliance. Some cloud-based implementations offer alerts that track regulatory changes in specific industries.

Among information governance stakeholders, GRC software is an enabling technology for risk management and compliance, as well as legal affairs, which must address legal issues that affect an organization's risk profile. As discussed in Part 1, a close relationship exists between risk management and compliance. The incident management component of GRC software is useful for information security.

Sensitive Data Finders

Organizations collect and maintain personally identifiable information, protected health information, payment card information, and other sensitive data for many purposes. Such data may be saved by multiple computer applications on a variety of storage devices. Determining the storage locations of sensitive data is the first step in protecting it from unauthorized access or inappropriate disclosure. As its name indicates, a sensitive data finder is an information security application that locates sensitive data in specified digital repositories. It uses specially developed algorithms that scan (search) a storage repository for content with characteristics indicative of sensitive data.

While other technologies, including file analysis and predictive coding, can identify sensitive data when performing file surveys or retrieval operations, sensitive data finders are optimized for that purpose. They provide a centralized, fully automated approach to the control and protection of sensitive information. While individual products vary, most sensitive data finders offer the following capabilities:

- ***Sensitive data finders can scan structured or unstructured digital content.*** The most versatile applications can locate sensitive information in databases, in data warehouses, on network or local hard drives, in electronic content management systems, in email archiving systems, or in repositories maintained by records management applications software. Some applications can also scan cloud-based repositories.

- ***Sensitive data finders are compatible with a variety of file formats for databases and digital documents.*** These formats include word processing files, spreadsheets, presentations, email, and web pages. Like automatic categorization, predictive coding, and other technologies previously discussed, sensitive data finders are limited to character-coded digital content. They cannot process digital photographs, video recordings, audio recordings, or other audiovisual information. Integrated optical character recognition capabilities are used to locate sensitive data in document images.

- ***Sensitive data finders can identify multiple types of numeric and alphanumeric information.*** This information may include a social security number, date of birth, credit card number, debit card number, bank account number, telephone number, password, passport number, or a driver's license number. Customers can also specify other numeric or alphanumeric data, such as student numbers or case numbers, with distinctive patterns.

- ***Storage repositories are scanned at specified intervals to identify new instances of sensitive data.*** Alternatively, some sensitive data finders monitor data traffic continuously to detect sensitive data in real-time as it is being collected and saved.

- ***Sensitive data finders highlight files that may require security action.*** When a file that contains sensitive data is discovered, authorized decision makers have several options. The file can be deleted, which is the best choice for obsolete data. The sensitive data can be redacted and the file retained. The file can be encrypted with password protection to prevent unauthorized access. The file can be moved to a protected location. If a file remains in place, it can be tagged so that the sensitive data finder will ignore it in subsequent scans.

Among information governance stakeholders, sensitive data finders are especially important for information security, risk management, compliance, and legal affairs. These stakeholders have significant responsibility for protecting sensitive information and preventing data breaches. Sensitive data finders can also prove useful for archival administration, which may need to restrict researcher's access to specific digital content, and for data science, which may need to identify and remove sensitive information prior to using specific digital content in analytical projects.

Data Anonymization Software

Data anonymization, sometimes described as data de-identification, is an information security technology that safeguards personal data. According to ISO/TS 25237, *Health informatics—Pseudonymization*, de-identification is a "general term for any process of removing the association between a set of identifying data and the data subject." As defined in ISO/IEC 29100, *Information technology—Security techniques—Privacy framework*, anonymization irreversibly alters personally identifiable information so that the data subject can no longer be identified, either directly or indirectly. In other words, anonymization modifies personal data to render it unrecognizable. If anonymization is successful, personal data cannot be linked to its original source.

Anonymization allows databases and digital documents that contain personal data to be used for secondary purposes—that is, for purposes other than the original purpose for which the personal data was created or collected. Common examples of secondary purposes include application development, modification, and testing projects, which require access to production databases that contain names, social security numbers, or other personal data. Anonymization is also required for research or analytical projects that involve digital content with personally identifiable information, protected health information, or payment card information. In these situations, the computer programmers, researchers, or other secondary users may not be authorized to access personal data, but they can utilize other information contained in a database or digital document collection. Anonymization can also be used to safeguard personal data stored on mobile devices, which may be lost or stolen; to exchange databases or digital documents with external entities; or to conceal personal data when database records or digital documents are retrieved.

Data anonymization is performed by computer algorithms that identify personal data. In this respect, data anonymization software shares some functionality with the sensitive data finders previously discussed, but anonymization software does not merely locate personal data, it modifies it as well. Typically, it produces a copy of a database or other digital content with the personal data obfuscated or removed. The original digital content remains intact. Sensitive data finders give authorized users the option of manually deleting or editing personal data, but anonymization software makes the changes automatically. It is optimized for that purpose. For their part, sensitive data finders are not limited to personal data; they can locate other types of confidential information. The two software categories are related but not interchangeable.

Data anonymization can be accomplished in several ways. Depending on the algorithm employed, the characteristics of the source data, and user requirements, data anonymization software may use one or more of the following methods:

- **Data masking.** Data masking alters social security numbers, payment card numbers, account numbers, telephone numbers, dates of birth, or other identifiers by replacing selected numbers with a masking character such as an X. In databases, the numbers to be masked are typically contained in designated fields. In digital documents, the numbers may be recognizable by their distinctive patterns.

- **Substitution.** Substitution replaces personal data with proxy data. Substitution can be used for numeric or alphabetic content. Personal names, for example, are replaced with different names; street addresses are replaced with different street addresses; telephone numbers are replaced with different telephone numbers; and so on. The new data values are typically selected from substitution lists.

- **Permutation or shuffling.** Permutation or shuffling replaces data in a given field of a database record with data from the same field in a different record within the same database. The data values are interchanged at random. Because personal data is not removed from the database, this approach may not provide sufficient security to satisfy all requirements.

- **Number variance.** The number variance approach modifies account numbers, dates of birth, height, weight, or other numerical data values by a random percentage within a predetermined range—plus or minus 20 percent or 30 days, for example. Thus, a date of birth of 12/2/1972 might be changed to 11/18/1974, or the account number 300383 might be changed to 264578, for example.

- **Redaction.** Redaction deletes personal data from database records or digital documents.

For information governance stakeholders, data anonymization addresses significant issues and concerns as follows:

- For information security, anonymization provides protection against data breaches.

- For data science, anonymization is a requirement for analytical projects, an important secondary use of digital content with personally identifiable information.

- For archival administration, anonymization may be required before certain databases and documents are made available for scholarly research.

- Risk management, compliance, and legal affairs are particularly concerned with anonymization requirements specified in laws and regulations. Most data protection laws, for example, follow the European Union model, which mandates anonymization to irreversibly prevent the identification of data subjects where databases or digital documents will be used for research purposes.

- Data anonymization is also necessary where digital content with personally identifiable information will be transferred to a country that does not provide an appropriate level of data protection.

- For medical research, a secondary use targeted by developers of data anonymization software, the HIPAA Privacy Rule requires de-identification of protected health information as a precondition for research projects involving patient records unless written authorization of the data subject is obtained. The HIPAA safe harbor method requires anonymization of all personal identifiers listed in 45 CFR 164.514. In academic institutions and research organizations, institutional review boards typically require an anonymization plan as a precondition for project approval.

Data Encryption Software

As defined in ISO/IEC 9798-1, *Information technology—Security techniques—Entity authentication—Part 1: General,* **data encryption** is a reversible transformation of data by a cryptographic algorithm to hide its information content. The purpose is to prevent unauthorized use of information. Cryptographic algorithms generate encryption keys that scramble data. Authorized users must have access to compatible decryption keys. Cryptographic algorithms and authentication mechanisms are covered by various standards, including ISO/IEC 18033-1, *Information technology—Security techniques—Encryption algorithms—Part 1: General,* ISO/IEC 18033-3, *Information technology—Security techniques—Encryption algorithms—Part 3: Block ciphers,* ISO/IEC 18033-4, *Information technology—Security techniques—Encryption algorithms—Part 3: Stream ciphers,* and ISO/IEC 19772, *Information technology—Security techniques—Authenticated encryption.*

Data encryption may be performed by software developed exclusively and optimized for that purpose. Alternatively, encryption functionality may be integrated into other software categories. Sensitive data finders, for example, may give authorized users the option of encrypting personal data or other confidential information once it is located. Similarly, some data anonymization applications allow authorized users to select encryption as a de-identification mechanism for personally identifiable information.

While capabilities vary from product to product, data encryption software offers some combination of the following features:

1. Data may be encrypted in storage, an approach described as encryption "at rest," or when it is being transferred, which is sometimes characterized as encryption "in motion."

2. Encryption of stored data can be applied to an entire hard drive—so-called whole disk encryption—or to selected folders or files. The whole disk approach encrypts the operating system and applications as well as user data. The Online Trust Alliance (OTA), a not-for-profit group that promotes trustworthy online practices, recommends whole-disk encryption for all laptops, mobile devices, and systems that host sensitive data.

3. Some encryption applications target a specific type of data—email, for example, which may be encrypted at the gateway server or client level. Secure Socket Layer (SSL) encryption is intended specifically for traffic between web browsers and servers. Always-on SSL is applied to an entire web session.

4. As an added layer of protection, some encryption software requires user authentication via a password or some other mechanism prior to decryption.

In addition to its obvious implications for information security, data encryption technology facilitates compliance with laws and regulations that require security precautions for specific types of information. Encryption can satisfy such requirements. The HIPAA Security Rule, for example, lists encryption as an addressable specification to safeguard protected health information. Addressable specifications allow a covered entity to employ other methods to accomplish the same purpose based on a reasonable analysis of risks, costs, and other factors. As specified in 12 CFR Part 364, *Appendix B—Interagency Guidelines for Establishing Information Security Standards*, the Federal Deposit Insurance Corporation (FDIC) requires banks to implement appropriate security measures for customer information in storage and transit. The regulations list encryption as an appropriate method. Requirement 3 of the Payment Card Industry Data Security Standard (PSS DSS) cites "strong cryptography" based on industry-tested algorithms as an appropriate method for secure storage of cardholder information. Many state laws include safe harbor provisions that exempt encrypted customer information data breach notification requirements.

Encryption technology is significant for other information governance stakeholders. For records management, encryption adds a layer of software dependence that can affect the continued usability of electronic records. Organizations must provide reasonable assurance that compatible decryption software will be available until retention periods for encrypted data elapse. For data science, encrypted data must be decrypted for use in analytical projects. For archival administration, permanent preservation of encrypted data requires the perpetual availability of compatible encryption software, a condition that is difficult to ensure. When security is no longer a concern, data will need to be permanently decrypted for scholarly use.

Data Destruction Software

ISO/TS 14265, *Health informatics—Classification of purposes for processing personal health information*, defines **data destruction** as an "operation that results in the permanent, unrecoverable removal of information…from memory or storage." According to ISO/IEC 27040, *Information technology—Security techniques—Storage security*, destruction ensures that "media cannot be reused as originally intended and that information is virtually impossible or prohibitively expensive to recover."

Destruction of digital content can be performed by hardware or software. Some hardware methods physically destroy media that contain classified information. According to DoD 5220.22M, *National Information Security Program: Operating Manual*, such methods include burning, shredding, pulping, melting, mutilation, chemical decomposition, or pulverizing. Sanitization is the process of removing data from media to permit reuse following eradication of data. NIST Special Publication 800-88, previously cited in Part 2, specifies requirements for media sanitization using hardware methods or software techniques. Hardware-based methods require equipment that is specifically designed for secure destruction of digital content. A degausser, for example, produces an intense magnetic field that erases hard drives or magnetic tapes. Degaussing is often followed by physical destruction of magnetic media. Special hardware is also available for physical destruction of solid-state devices or nonerasable optical media.

As an alternative to degaussing and physical destruction, data destruction software permits reuse of hard drives or magnetic tapes following erasure. While features and functions vary from product to product, data destruction software supports the following capabilities:

1. Data destruction software can delete the entire contents of a given medium, including applications as well as data or selected information, specific folders or files that are recorded on a hard drive, for example.

2. The data destruction process overwrites digital content with a random stream of bits. When data is overwritten, data recovery methods cannot be used to reconstruct files. Verification algorithms determine that digital content is properly overwritten.

3. Most data destruction applications comply with DoD 5220.22M or other specifications issued by government agencies or security organizations. Examples include the Canadian RCMP TSSIT OPS-II specification, the British CSEC ITSG-06 specification, the German VSITR specification, and the New Zealand NZSIT 402 specification. Some data destruction applications can be customized to overwrite data multiple times, although multipass erasure can be time consuming.

4. To maintain an audit trail, data destruction software produces data destruction logs or reports that identify the media involved, the sanitization method, the number of overwriting passes performed, and the number of bad sectors encountered.

5. Some data destruction software generates a certificate attesting that a given medium has been securely erased.

The ability to destroy data securely is a requirement for any information governance initiative that involves confidential information. Secure data destruction is a critical aspect of information security and risk management, and it is essential for compliance with laws and regulations that mandate secure destruction of personally identifiable information, protected health information, and payment card information. For records management, secure data destruction plays a critical role in the implementation of retention schedules.

Summary of Major Points

- ☑ Enabling technologies facilitate the completion of tasks or activities that would otherwise be difficult or impossible to perform. Certain technologies play an enabling role in information governance.

- ☑ Enterprise content management, digital asset management, physical records management software, file analysis software, automatic document categorization, master data management, and collaborative software are enabling technologies that can organize, categorize, and analyze information.

- ☑ Records management application software, email archiving software, digital preservation software, web archiving, social media archiving, and file conversion software are enabling technologies that manage the lifecycle of digital content.

- ☑ Full text indexing and searching, federated searching, predictive coding, and e-discovery software are enabling technologies for information retrieval.

- ☑ GRC software, sensitive data finders, data anonymization software, data encryption software, and data destruction software are enabling technologies that support risk management and information security functions.

Table 1

Comparison of Governance Models

	Executive Centered	Policy Governance	Collaboration Governance	Working Board	Advisory Board
Who selects board members?	Executive	Practices vary	Stakeholder units	Stakeholder units	Executive
Who sets the board's agenda?	Executive	Governing board	Governing board	Governing board	Executive
Who defines strategic direction?	Executive with board input	Governing board	Governing board	Governing board	Executive, possibly with board input
Is governance distinct from management?	No	Yes	Yes	No	Yes
Is strong executive required?	Yes	No	No	No	Yes
Is board independent of executive?	No	Yes	Yes	Yes	No
Is board involved in operations?	No	No	No	Yes	No

Table 2

Responsibility Assignment Matrix

A= Accountable
R=Responsible
C=Consulted
I=Informed

	Records Mgmt	Info Tech	Info Security	Risk Mgmt	Compliance	Legal Affairs	Data Science	Archival Admin
Develop policies, rules, and guidelines that satisfy requirements for retention of recorded information	A,R	C	C	C	C	C	C	C
Develop policies and standards for retention formats, media, and locations	A,R	C	C	C	C	C	C	C
Develop policies and processes for defensible disposition of obsolete information	A,R	C	C	C	C	C		
Develop guidelines and processes for efficient management of inactive physical records	A,R		C	C	C	I		C
Recommend technologies and processes for organization and retrieval of information	A,R	C		I	I	I	C	C
Develop protection and disaster recovery plans for mission-critical physical records	A,R		C	C	C	I		I
Evaluate, acquire, and implement computing and networking components and services	C	A,R	C	C	C	C	C	C
Optimize utilization of technological resources for storage and processing of digital information	C	A,R	I				I	C
Implement technologies and processes for continued accessibility and reliability of digital information	C	A,R	I	C	C	I	I	C
Implement controls to prevent unauthorized access to digital information	I	A,R	C	C	C	C	I	I
Implement processes to identify and delete obsolete digital information as defined by retention policies	C	A,R	C	C	C	C	I	I
Provide backup protection and disaster recovery capability for digital information	I	A,R	C	C	C	C	I	I
Develop policies and processes to prevent unauthorized disclosure and other security lapses	I	C	A,R	C	C	I	I	I
Respond to and investigate security events involving information resources	I	C	A,R	C	C	C	I	I

Table 2

Responsibility Assignment Matrix (continued)

A= Accountable
R=Responsible
C=Consulted
I=Informed

	Records Mgmt	Info Tech	Info Security	Risk Mgmt	Compliance	Legal Affairs	Data Science	Archival Admin
Evaluate and recommend equipment, software, and services to protect information	I	C	A,R	C	I	I	I	I
Identify information resources that require special security arrangements	C	C	A,R	C	C	C	C	C
Develop policies and processes for secure destruction of obsolete information resources	C	C	A,R	C	C	C	I	I
Identify, evaluate, and monitor internal risks that threaten information resources	C	C	C	A,R	C	C	I	C
Identify, evaluate, and monitor external events that threaten information resources	C	C	C	A,R	C	C	I	C
Develop plans, policies, and processes to anticipate, mitigate, transfer, or eliminate risks	C	C	C	A,R	C	C	C	C
Direct, coordinate, and monitor responses to specific information-related risks	C	C	C	A,R	C	C	I	C
Review information-related policies and practices for alignment with compliance requirements	C	C	C	C	A,R	C	I	C
Identify, monitor, and issue alerts about legal and regulatory developments	I	I	I	I	A,R	C	I	I
Monitor information-related activities for compliance with internal and external mandates	I	I	C	C	A,R	C	I	I
Provide advice, assistance, and interpretations about compliance-related matters	I	I	I	I	A,R	C	I	I
Conduct inquiries and investigations into possible compliance violations	C	C	C	C	A,R	C		
Assemble information for submissions to regulatory authorities	C	C			A,R	C		
Serve as contact point for inquiries or other interactions with regulatory authorities					A,R	C		
Align information-related policies, procedures, and practices with legal requirements	C	C	C	C	C	A,R	C	C

Table 2

Responsibility Assignment Matrix (continued)

A= Accountable
R=Responsible
C=Consulted
I=Informed

	Records Mgmt	Info Tech	Info Security	Risk Mgmt	Compliance	Legal Affairs	Data Science	Archival Admin
Provide legal opinions and interpretations about laws and regulations related to information	C	C	C	C	C	A,R	I	I
Issue holds to preserve information deemed relevant for legal proceedings	C	C	I	C	I	A,R	I	I
Perform or coordinate information-related discovery for legal proceedings	C	C	I	C	C	A,R	C	I
Define policies and procedures for analyzing data, including privacy and data protection issues	C	C	C	C	C	C	A,R	
Identify information needed for specific analytical projects and activities	C	C	C	I	C	C	A,R	C
Collect and convert information from existing data sets		C	C	C			A,R	
Identify information with continuing value for historical or scholarly purposes	C	C		C	C			A,R
Develop policies and standards for permanent preservation of archival information	I	C		C	C	C	I	A,R
Evaluate and implement technologies and processes for archival information	I	C	C	C			I	A,R

Table 3

Stakeholder Impact Matrix

	Records Mgmt	Info Tech	Info Security	Risk Mgmt	Compliance	Legal Affairs	Data Science	Archival Admin
Information creation/collection requirements	✓			✓	✓	✓		
Records retention requirements	✓	✓		✓	✓	✓		
Mandatory destruction requirements	✓	✓	✓	✓	✓	✓		
Electronic recordkeeping requirements	✓	✓	✓	✓	✓	✓		✓
Data residency requirements	✓	✓		✓	✓	✓		
Data protection and privacy requirements	✓	✓	✓	✓	✓	✓	✓	✓
Security planning requirements	✓	✓	✓	✓	✓	✓	✓	✓
Data disposal requirements	✓	✓	✓	✓	✓	✓	✓	✓
Data breach notification requirements			✓	✓	✓	✓		
Information backup requirements	✓	✓	✓	✓	✓	✓		
Required disclosure by government agencies	✓	✓	✓	✓	✓	✓	✓	✓
Required disclosure to government agencies	✓	✓	✓	✓	✓	✓		
Mandatory public notification			✓	✓	✓	✓		
Court-ordered disclosure	✓	✓	✓	✓	✓	✓		✓
Prohibited disclosure of nonpersonal information				✓	✓	✓		
Statutes of limitations	✓			✓	✓	✓	✓	

Table 4

Technology Impact Matrix

	Records Mgmt	Info Tech	Info Security	Risk Mgmt	Compliance	Legal Affairs	Data Science	Archival Admin
Enterprise content management	✓	✓	✓	✓	✓	✓	✓	
Digital asset management	✓	✓	✓	✓	✓	✓	✓	✓
Physical records management software	✓	✓	✓	✓	✓	✓		✓
File analysis software	✓	✓	✓	✓	✓	✓		✓
Automatic document categorization	✓	✓		✓	✓	✓	✓	✓
Master data management	✓	✓	✓	✓	✓	✓	✓	✓
Records management application software	✓	✓	✓	✓	✓	✓	✓	✓
Email archiving software	✓	✓	✓	✓	✓	✓	✓	✓
Digital preservation software	✓	✓	✓	✓	✓		✓	✓
Social media archiving	✓	✓		✓	✓	✓	✓	✓
File conversion software	✓	✓		✓	✓	✓	✓	✓
Federated search	✓	✓	✓	✓	✓	✓	✓	✓
Predictive coding	✓	✓	✓	✓	✓	✓	✓	✓
E-discovery software		✓	✓	✓	✓	✓		
GRC software		✓	✓	✓	✓	✓		
Sensitive data finders		✓	✓	✓	✓	✓	✓	✓
Data anonymization software		✓	✓	✓	✓	✓	✓	✓
Data encryption software		✓	✓	✓	✓	✓	✓	✓
Data destruction software	✓	✓	✓	✓	✓	✓		

Glossary of Terms

The following list contains brief definitions of selected terms used in this book. Except for a few grammatical changes, the definitions are identical to those presented in the sections where the terms are introduced. Some entries are adapted from definitions presented in international standards. The relevant portions of individual sections should be consulted for a fuller explanation and discussion of specific terms. This glossary is provided for the reader's convenience. It is neither a comprehensive list of information governance terms nor is it intended as a substitute for other general or specialized glossaries.

A – D

asset. An item, thing, or entity that has potential or value to an organization.

automatic document categorization. Technology that assigns digital documents to predefined categories based on their contents and other characteristics.

business process management. A disciplined approach to identify, design, execute, document, measure, monitor, and control automated and nonautomated business processes.

compliance. A control function concerned with meeting an organization's obligations and requirements.

data anonymization. The process of removing the association between a set of identifying data and the data subject.

data breach. A compromise of security that leads to accidental or unlawful access to or destruction, loss, alteration, or unauthorized disclosure of protected data.

data destruction. An operation that results in the permanent, unrecoverable removal of information.

data encryption. A reversible transformation of data by a cryptographic algorithm to hide its information content.

data governance. The exercise of authority, control, and shared decision making over the management of data assets.

data protection laws. Laws that regulate the collection, use, and distribution of personally identifiable information.

data residency laws. Laws that specify the geographic locations where specific information can be stored.

data science. An interdisciplinary field that employs a combination of statistics, mathematics, computer modeling, data visualization, pattern recognition, and machine learning to explore, extract, and analyze digital information.

data sovereignty. A concept that recognizes that an organization's information-related policies and practices must comply with legal and regulatory requirements in all locations where it does business.

data subject. A person about whom information is maintained.

digital asset management (DAM). Technology designed for storage, cataloging, indexing, retrieval, distribution, and protection of visual and audio content.

digital preservation. Technology that ensures long-term integrity and usability of digital documents and other unstructured digital content of permanent value.

discovery. The investigative phase of litigation when opposing parties can obtain information to help them prepare for trial.

E – G

e-discovery. Legal discovery that involves electronically stored information.

email archiving system. Software that creates and maintains a repository for retention of messages and their associated attachments transferred from an organization's email system.

enterprise content management (ECM). Technology that creates and maintains an organized, searchable repository of digital documents and other unstructured digital content.

federated country. A sovereign state in which the national government shares legislative and regulatory authority with subnational jurisdictions.

federated search. Technology that performs retrieval operations on multiple content repositories simultaneously.

file conversion. The process of transforming digital content from one file format to another.

freedom of information laws. Laws that give the public the right to request information held by government agencies.

full-text indexing. Computerized indexing method for digital documents; allows documents to be retrieved by the words or phrases they contain.

governance. The action or manner of governing in the sense of directing and controlling with the authority of a superior; the way that an entity is controlled by the people who run it.

governance framework. Strategies, policies, decision-making structures, and accountabilities through which an organization's governance arrangements operate.

governance, risk management, and compliance (GRC). An umbrella discipline that combines governance, risk management, and compliance.

I – M

information assurance. An aspect of risk management that is specifically concerned with strategic and operational risks associated with creation, collection, processing, storage, use, and distribution of information.

information governance. A strategic, cross-disciplinary framework of standards, processes, roles, and metrics that hold organizations and individuals accountable for the proper handling of information assets. The framework helps organizations achieve business objectives, facilitates compliance with external requirements, and minimizes risk posed by sub-standard information handling practices.

information security. The preservation of confidentiality, authenticity, reliability, and availability of information.

information security governance. The system by which an organization's information security activities are directed and controlled.

innovation governance. A framework and process to promote organizational effectiveness through innovation.

internal controls. Ongoing tasks and activities that provide reasonable assurance regarding achievement of an organization's objectives relating to operations, reporting, and compliance.

IT governance. The system by which the current and future use of information technology is directed and controlled.

master data hub. An enterprise-wide replacement for decentralized databases that are created, maintained, and utilized by specific applications.

master data management. An aspect of data governance that is concerned with creating and maintaining authoritative reference data.

maturity model. An analytical tool for planning, assessing, and advancing a strategic initiative by measuring the maturity of an activity, operation, or business process.

P – W

personally identifiable information. Any information that can be used to identify an individual directly or indirectly.

predictive coding. Technology that combines linguistic analysis with statistical calculations to identify digital documents that satisfy specific retrieval requirements.

principled performance. The ability to reliably achieve objectives while addressing uncertainty and acting with integrity.

process governance. Discipline that focuses, analyzes, and coordinates an organization's process management initiatives and activities.

project governance. A subset of corporate governance activities that are specifically related to project activities.

recordkeeping requirements. Laws, regulations, or other legal instruments that require organizations to create, collect, and retain records related to business activities and operations.

records management application. Software that creates and maintains a reliable repository for retention of digital documents and other digital content.

risk. The effect of uncertainty on objectives, often expressed as a combination of the adverse consequences of an event and the likelihood of occurrence of the event.

risk governance. Activity that applies governance concepts to the identification, categorization, assessment, management, evaluation, and communication of risks.

risk management. Coordinated activities to direct and control an organization with regard to risk.

social media archiving. Technology that collects, indexes, and saves information that an organization posts on publicly accessible social media sites.

stakeholder. A business unit or functional area that is involved with or affected by an organization's information-related strategies, policies, or processes.

statutes of limitations. Laws that define the period of time during which legal proceedings related to specific matters must commence.

unitary state. A sovereign state governed as a single entity.

valuation. The process of estimating what an asset is worth in monetary terms.

web archiving. Technology that collects and preserves the content and appearance of websites on the public Internet or organizational intranets.

Suggestions for Further Study and Research

A large and growing number of books, articles, conference papers, and other publications contain more detailed or otherwise different treatments of topics covered in this book. While a comprehensive bibliography is beyond the purpose and scope of this book, this appendix provides some suggestions for further reading and research.

Library catalogs, which are searchable at library websites, are the best resources for citations to books and monographs about information governance. Large national and academic libraries are likely to have the most complete holdings. The Library of Congress Online Catalog and the OCLC WorldCat database, which combines the holdings of thousands of libraries, are good starting points. Both are searchable online at no charge. While "information governance" is not a Library of Congress subject heading, the phrase does appear in the titles of a growing number of books, and it is also the case for related governance initiatives.

Various business indexes and databases contain citations to articles about information governance in professional journals, popular periodicals, and newspapers. Examples of online databases likely to be available in many medium-size and larger academic and public libraries include ABI Inform, EBSCO Business Sources Complete, and Factiva. Records management publications are also indexed in library science and technical databases, including Library, Information Science and Technology Abstracts (LISTA), Library and Information Science Abstracts (LISA), Ei Compendex, Inspec, Web of Science, and Scopus. Articles indexed in these databases range from brief overviews of information governance concepts and issues to detailed case studies that describe information governance initiatives in specific companies, government agencies, and other organizations.

Bibliographic and ordering information for international standards cited in this book is available online at *www.iso.org*. All laws and regulations cited in Part 3 are available online at no charge.

Google and other search engines are obvious starting points to locate pertinent websites about information governance concepts, requirements, technologies, and related topics, but the voluminous results they deliver can require time-consuming browsing. The websites of professional associations and industry groups are valuable sources of information about many of the topics discussed in this book. Examples include ARMA International, the Information Governance Initiative, AIIM, the American Health Information Management Association (AHIMA), The Sedona Conference®, the Society of American Archivists, the Archives & Records Association (ARA), the Data Governance Professionals Organization (DGPO), DAMA International, the Information Coalition, the Enterprise Information Management Institute (EIMI), ISACA, the Risk Management Society (RIMS), the Institute of Risk Management (IRM), the National Society of Compliance Professionals (NSCP), the Society of Corporate Compliance and Ethics, and the International Association of Risk and Compliance Professionals (IARCP).

Index

About the Author

William Saffady, Ph.D., is a records and information management specialist based in New York City. He is the author of over three dozen books and many articles on electronic records retention, digital document management, storage and preservation of recorded information, and other records and information management topics. Recent books by Dr. Saffady published by ARMA International include *Legal Requirements for Electronic Records Retention in Asia, Legal Requirements for Electronic Records Retention in Western Europe, Legal Requirements for Electronic Records Retention in Eastern Europe, E-Mail Retention and Archiving: Issues and Guidance for Compliance and Discovery, Records and Information Management: Fundamentals of Professional Practice*, 3rd edition, and *Cost Analysis Concepts and Methods for Records Management Projects*, 2nd edition. In addition to research and writing, Dr. Saffady serves as an information management consultant, providing analytical services and training to corporations, government agencies, not-for-profit entities, cultural institutions, and other organizations.

About ARMA International

ARMA International is a not-for-profit professional association and the authority on governing information as a strategic asset. Established in 1955, the association's approximate 27,000+ members include information governance professionals, archivists, corporate librarians, imaging specialists, legal professionals, IT managers, consultants, and educators, all of whom work in a variety of industries, including government, legal, healthcare, financial services, and petroleum in the United States, Canada, and more than 30 countries around the globe.

ARMA International's mission is to provide informational professionals the resources, tools, and training they need to effectively manage records and information within an established information governance framework.

The ARMA International headquarters office is located in Overland Park, Kansas, in the Kansas City metropolitan area. Office hours are 8:30 a.m. to 5:00 p.m. (CT), Monday through Friday.

ARMA International
11880 College Blvd., Suite 450
Overland Park, KS 66210
913.341.3808
Fax: 913.341.3742

headquarters@armaintl.org
www.arma.org

Printed in the USA
CPSIA information can be obtained
at www.ICGtesting.com
LVHW081112191023
761560LV00009B/332